THE AXLE OF THE YEAR

BILL DUVENDACK

All rights reserved,
no part of this publication
may be reproduced or transmitted by any
means whatsoever without the prior
permission of the publisher.

Edited by Toni Glitz
glitzedit.co.uk

Text © Bill Duvendack

ISBN 978-1-916756-30-4

Veneficia Publications

NOVEMBER 2024

VENEFICIA PUBLICATIONS UK
veneficiapublications.com

This book is dedicated to the Dolmen –
however you understand it.

CONTENTS

INTRODUCTION i

CHAPTER ONE 1

CHAPTER TWO 27

CHAPTER THREE 67

CHAPTER FOUR 93

CHAPTER FIVE 113

CHAPTER SIX 137

CHAPTER SEVEN 159

APPENDIX I I

APPENDIX II XIX

APPENDIX III XXII

APPENDIX IV XXXI

APPENDIX V XLV

BIBLIOGRAPHY LI

INTRODUCTION

There are many books on the market about what is commonly called The Wheel of the Year, or The Witches' Year, so what makes this one any different? This book is not just a look at the wheel of the year, it is also a working manual for understanding it.

While it is very easy to regurgitate information from various cultures and traditions, it is far harder to demonstrate the details, such as the Whys and Hows. It is much more common to find books that are collections of correspondences and compiled histories. Both of those subjects are very valuable and I encourage you to seek them out if desired, however, they are not the focal point of this work.

This work looks at the underpinnings of the magical year. I have decided to use the word 'axle' in the title because we are not discussing every festival in depth or detail, rather, we will be looking at the energetic, metaphysical, and astrological underpinnings behind them. In order to do this, we will also look at rarely discussed topics as astrotheology and astromythology. In other words, we will deal extensively with theory and extrapolation.

Part of this will entail looking at various astrological patterns that occur around the times of the festivals, so you don't get surprised by a disruptive influence.

You could consider this a What-To-Expect manual. It is a collection of articles I have written over the years for the digital magazine *Dolmen Grove Chronicles*, later renamed *Dolmen Chronicles* – a collection spanning several years. What is included here are astrological insights and observations that coincide with these sacred Earth festivals. Updating things to the twenty-first century, I will be taking a different approach to what is commonly found. In the appendix there are two new articles that pertain to the topics in here.

Instead of simply listing the eight festivals and discussing them one at a time, I have paired them with their opposite festival. I have done this because the planet is more interconnected than ever, and what is true in the northern hemisphere at one time of the year is not true during the same time of the year in the southern. Specifically, when one hemisphere is celebrating one festival, the other hemisphere is celebrating the opposite. Hence the chapters are laid out in an axis fashion.

As well as discussing the festivals, we will also look at other celestial topics. For example, the article

Born of Heat and Light is a fairly comprehensive look at angels and the history of how they came to be as they are commonly understood today. A few articles in here will also look at basic metaphysics for the sake of understanding the flow of energy from a metaphysical perspective.

When you consider these points, you see that in a lot of ways, this is a How-To manual when it comes to understanding the energies present during the year. This is another point that separates this book from others, because generalities and principles will be scrutinized, and whether you accept the information or reject it in favor of what you already know, you will leave this book with a more comprehensive understanding of the nature and flow of energy across the planet and throughout the year. Patterns will be revealed, as well as insights into astrology.

Don't worry, this is not a primer on astrology, but rather a glimpse into what astrology addresses and teaches – the exchanges and interactions that impact us all of the time on the planet we all share.

Whatever your reason for picking this book up, I hope you find the information in here useful and enlightening. Through applying this material, you can bring yourself into greater alignment with the energy of the seasons, thereby removing a lot of the need to memorize specific details of each festival, although I still encourage you to do that. By working with this material, you will hopefully come away with a deeper understanding of the connectedness of all things, and how to resonate with natural energies that have long been ignored by the modern person.

CHAPTER ONE
ARCHAEOASTRONOMY, ASTROMYTHOLOGY, AND ASTROTHEOLOGY

It may sound like we are going to discuss a lot here, but we're really not. As mentioned in the introduction, none of these three topics get as much attention as they should, in my opinion, when it comes to occultism and modern spirituality. I find this ironic because all three are basically the underpinnings of civilization. Humanity has been working with these themes, albeit without these specific titles, dating back to the earliest times before recorded history. All around the world we find ancient stone structures that are aligned with various celestial phenomenon, so we know for a fact that our most ancient ancestors placed a lot of emphasis on the sky, which completely makes sense.

To illustrate this fascination, go and stand outside. When you look around, you will see the world is split into two halves – the flat plane of the Earth and the sky. Such a simple observation tells us what our ancestors saw, and what has influenced us most as a species.

The idea of aligning structures and even beliefs with the stars has been well discussed and documented over the centuries but it is only in the last several decades that terms and categorizations have been created and applied. This is why the subjects are not as widely known about as I feel they should be. Bluntly put, they are new subject titles for centuries-old interests. Many people know that Stonehenge, for example, aligns with the solstices and lunar cycles, however, far fewer people know that the term for studying this sacred site and those like it is called archaeoastronomy. This is not a criticism of those who don't know the term, rather it simply illustrates the point I am making.

It is because of this disconnect that this chapter exists. In here I will unveil the three subjects listed above to help you realize that what you already know has modern terms and classifications. This will make it easier to find information that interests you. And, as it applies to the rest of the book, this information can help you understand how powerful ancient Earth festivals are, energetically speaking. When you choose to work with any or all of these festivals you are tapping into a current of energy that has been developed and worked with for centuries. Through this alignment, you can increase the results of your work and align with the greater reality we all share.

To use a phrase, you align the micro of the self with the macro of the cosmos, and all of those who have come before have done the same. Enough of the preliminaries, let's begin!

Archaeoastronomy And Astroarchaeology

The first of these topics we will discuss will continue the conversation about Stonehenge that we started above. A detail should be noted here, which is that these terms are very new. According to dictionary.com, these terms date back to the 1970s, and upon further investigation, we find that the two terms are effectively interchangeable. There is a slight difference between the words, of course, so let's take a slight detour to discuss that.

As you have probably deduced, archaeoastronomy is a combination of archaeo and astronomy. Archaeo comes from ancient Greek and means ancient. If you're familiar with my other books and courses, then you know that astronomy essentially means the naming of stars, and includes both the naming of stars and their categorization. When we put the two halves together, we arrive at a definition: The study of ancient star related sites. When it comes to astroarchaeology, we have the same essence: The study of star related archaeology. These are my definitions, and you will find other definitions if you look in other places. I am keeping these definitions simple and direct because there are nuanced differences in the field of academia, where the terms are predominantly used. For us lay people, these will suffice for now.

The remains of all sites on Earth that were created long ago and built to align with certain celestial events fall into this category. Most of the sites that fall under this umbrella were created thousands of years ago, specifically during the Paleolithic era. For context, the Paleolithic era is the age that ends just around the time of the most recent ice age. This means that most of these sites are twelve thousand years old or so, give or take two thousand years. If sites do not fall into this category, then they were built in the Neolithic age. As many of you know, neo means new, so this period follows the Paleolithic. Specifically, this encompasses the period from 10000 BCE (Before Common Era) to as recent as 2000 BCE. If you are familiar with ancient history, then you know just how much happened during this period. Many of the well-known ancient civilizations date to this time, such as the Egyptians and Mesopotamians.

To show how prevalent this subject is today, the existence of these sites prove that humanity has been around for a lot longer than conservative history teaches us. For example, the fertile crescent part of the world is generally known as the cradle of civilization and is located between the Tigris and Euphrates rivers. Remains of structures obviously built by humans date back to before the most recent ice age, which means that people have been congregating and building structures for far longer than what is taught in school about the fertile crescent. The only difference between Paleolithic structures and the fertile crescent is that before the ice age, people did not congregate in what would develop into towns and later cities. People were more nomadic and only made special trips to these structures. Some humans lived there but they were not nexus points for large groups. A collection of structures regularly inhabited by humans was a new invention in the fertile crescent, which means that it is contextually recent in human social evolution. We have been a nomadic species for much longer than we have been congregating in population centers. That is a conversation for another time and for now we will return to our topic.

Hence, when we are talking about astroarchaeology, we are talking about really old things. While we know now they were built in celestial alignment, there is no written record of the people who built them. All we know is that their architects were not only aware of the connection between us and the cosmos, they saw value in honoring out-of-the-ordinary celestial events.

Some of the structures show impressive architectural techniques that cannot be replicated today without the use of high-end technology, making their creation that much more impressive.

The science behind this is worth understanding, too, although only on a superficial level because of the focus of this book. Not only do astroarchaeologists look at the age of the structures, they also look at their composition, and through excavations, any surviving artifacts found at those locations. These artifacts range from broken shards of pottery all the way to actual human remains, no matter how miniscule they might be. Various dating processes, such as carbon-14 dating, are used, and really, this is where I will draw the line on the subject. I'm smart enough to know there are various processes and techniques, not smart enough to know all of them, and lazy enough to not learn them.

It is also worth mentioning here that we technically do not know who built these structures. At the time they were built, both homo sapiens and Neanderthals coexisted.

Recent discoveries have even revealed that they intermingled, and Neanderthal genes can still be found in blood today. There is a lot of information about this particular subject that can be found, and I tread lightly here because I am not an expert in those fields, however, I know they are worth investigating if you feel compelled. Some of the oldest sites, such as Göbekli Tepe, may have been built by Homo Sapiens, or they could have been built by Neanderthals. We should not be so full of pride to assume they were built by Homo Sapiens. For example, some of the stones that were used to build the oldest sacred sites are larger than stones used more recently, which could imply that a larger-built type of bipedal built them. Regardless of who built them, it is worth keeping in mind that each site is mathematically constructed, which means that mathematics as we know it today has been around a lot longer than Pythagoras. You have to work with mathematic principles, such as geometry, to construct a site that only aligns with the sun or moon a few times a year.

While it is debatable whether or not Göbekli Tepe is astronomical in creation and usage, another location, Nabta Playa in Egypt, is not debatable. Known as the world's oldest astronomical calendar, it is also the oldest standing stone circle in the world, predating Stonehenge by thousands of years.

I wrote about the site in my book *A Draconian Egyptian Grimoire*, so I will not go into great depth about it here.

I will share key points from that piece to illustrate our point here to put it into context of this book.

Nabta Playa is located in southern Egypt in the deep desert. When it was functional and populated, the area was a lush, rich green land.

*

Excerpt from *A Draconian Egyptian Grimoire*, Duvendack, 2019

At that site, there are standing stones and stones that once were standing, in a similar concept to Stonehenge. These stones have been determined to line up to two different astronomical phenomena, interestingly enough. On one hand, it can be argued that the stones tracked the movements of the stars Sirius, Arcturus, Alpha Centauri, and even the constellation Orion.

However, there is another astronomical feature present. Another theory states that the way a lot of the stones are aligned, they are actually showing a representation of the heliacal rising of the Galactic Center on spring equinox as it was in approximately 17500 BCE!

Of course, this implies it is much older than the accepted dates of 6000 BCE. I have looked at the evidence and from my interpretation of it, that is probably the more accurate date for the use of that site on a regular basis for ceremonial reasons. Don't take my word for it though, please do the research and see what you uncover.

Another part of this puzzle is that some of the stones correspond to how the Milky Way is viewed from the northern galactic pole. If this theory is correct, it puts the date of approximately 17500 BCE as the true origins of the gods of Egypt, and it would all start with Het-Hoor. Interestingly enough, a cow plays a prominent role in another western spiritual tradition, that of the Norse, however that is a conversation for another time.

Finally, the other detail to factor in is that at the believed construction time of Nabta Playa, it was built on the Tropic of Cancer, which was the sun's farthest point north until it shifted many years later. Even if you subscribe to the dates of 6100 BCE – 5600 BCE, this still solidifies many things, and for context, the mighty cities and urban centers of Sumeria were still approximately 1,500 years in the future.

Another part of the picture of Nabta Playa to consider is that some of the stones found there represent the stars on Orion's belt at two of their distinct stations in the sky.

One set of stones represents the three stars of Orion's belt when they are at their minimum tilt in the sky when you look at them. Another set of stones matches the stars found in the shoulder and head of the constellation at maximum tilt. So, effectively in the opposite position. The stones corresponding to the maximum tilt date back to approximately 16500 BCE, which is about 100 years after the depiction of the Milky Way via the stones. For reference, the cycle between minimum and maximum tilts takes approximately 25,000 years. What this means is that it is theoretically possible that this location has been in use for more than 25,000 years, or at least tracked the movements of the stars over that great expanse of time, so if the site wasn't being used to track the stars all of that time, then it was intermittently used, which is still profound.

*

Göbekli Tepe and Nabta Playa are only two prime examples of archaeoastronomy – there are many, especially newer, examples, such as Stonehenge. I hope these brief overviews illustrate what this subject looks at and how it ties into the axle of the year. All three of these locations illustrate the fact that humans have been celebrating seasonal changes and celestial alignments. These are the roots of the wheel of the year as we know it today.

This does mean everything dates back to Egypt but that is a conversation for another time and place.

Astromythology

Astromythology is related to archaeoastronomy, and they are discussed in the same conversations, usually regarding the same topics, however, they are different on a technical point. Often, astromythology is lumped together with our third and final topic, astrotheology, however, I am separating them here for the sake of clarity and to be technical. Two parts of the word, astro and myth, reveal what this subject covers. We've already discussed what astro means, which leaves us with the word mythology to clarify.

According to dictionary.com, the word mythology means a body of myths, as that of a particular people or that relate to a particular person. This gives us two important points. First, mythology can apply to a group of characters that are usually tied to a particular culture or people. For example, Egyptian mythology, which contains the stories of ancient Egypt as well as the stories of Horus. Second, mythology can apply to specifically one character. For example, the mythology of Horus from ancient Egypt.

Another part of mythology that we will discuss later is the difference between personal mythology and the more objective mythologies we are referencing here. Just like cultures have their myths, individual people have their myths, too.

If you have been paying close attention, then you know in the above section I discussed the astronomical side of ancient sites but I did not discuss the mythologies associated with them. I gave you a hint with the mention of Het Hoor in the reprint from *A Draconian Egyptian Grimoire*. While sacred sites align with celestial phenomenon, they also generally have myths, stories, and characters associated with them as well. Nabta Playa corresponds to Het Hoor, commonly known as Hathor, as is evidenced by the remains of cattle sacrifice. This makes her one of the oldest goddesses on the planet, being dwarfed only by the age of Venus of Willendorf (although not the goddess, Venus. She came into being thousands of years later) and the Nile goddess, also known as Bat. She requires some conversation because really, she was the first Egyptian cow goddess before Hathor, and her characteristics were consumed by the growing Hathor cult. This does mean that she was probably the one associated with Nabta Playa, but I stuck with Hathor because of her fame. Anyway, back to our discussion.

Astromythology is found all across the globe, and it is a well-established fact that many ancient cultures have deities that correspond to such places as the sun, moon, and other local planets of our solar system. Aligning stories and characters with planets, stars and moons is astromythology in its purest sense, even though we may not think of it. How these beings relate to celestial bodies and the cycles of our planet is quite common, so common to the degree that most people don't even know there is a formalized field of study addressing these common traits. Essentially, this is where Jungian archetypes come into being. If culture X has a sun god and culture Y has one, too, then by default, and through common sense, we can see there are strong parallels between them and they usually share common traits.

There are differences unique to each culture, and this should not be ignored, but by and large there are far more traits that are shared than are different.

The existence of astromythology also implies that there is mythology that is not celestial in orientation. Deities and spirits that are not astromythological in nature include earth gods and goddesses such as the Green Man, Pan, Dionysus, and Gaia. Pluto, Neptune, and Lakshmi all come to mind as more examples.

I mention this point here to dissuade you from thinking that all deities and spirits fall into the category of astromythology. While many deities do, there are a great number of deities that don't. Critical thinking and knowing the myths can help to identify who goes where, so to speak. I encourage you to apply this line of thinking to your work as you progress along the path.

A slight divergence is necessary to clarify something. When these sites were active, they usually aligned with celestial events, as discussed previously, but at that time there was no difference between astrology and astronomy. The subject would just be considered 'star stuff', to coin a phrase.

Astronomy didn't exist as we know it, then again, neither did astrology. Astronomy and astrology are flip sides of the same coin, although neither as we know them today were practiced. What this means is that there was the sun, moon, solstices, equinoxes, and some star constellations. The planets were known about, but most of the sacred sites we're discussing did not align with them as much as they did the aforementioned phenomena. Hence the planets were secondary in importance and some celestial locations and events that were used then are no longer considered important.

A great example of this is the constellation Draco at the North Pole. For thousands of years, it was tracked and worshipped, however, you won't find it in any prominent astrological texts of today, nor astronomical work, either. Essentially this means that it is a sleeping giant, energetically speaking – the energy still remains. It is dwindling the longer it is not appreciated, although currently it is still there to utilize. The age of the structures that fall into these categories predate any modern system of classification and understanding. I point this out because in academia today these are called astronomical sites, however that is not entirely accurate. It is just as correct to call them astrological sites.

Another point to consider is the source of the alignments. Some liberal thinkers speculate that ancient people received the knowledge of these divine alignments and their potency from aliens and other such arcane sources, but as I clarified before, that is not necessarily correct. Modern people make mistakes and jump to conclusions when there are perfectly reasonable explanations, namely that many people over many generations passed information related to the stars and sacred alignments one to another, and thus created a succession of truth that was predominantly oral rather than written.

This is noteworthy because more of human history has been transmitted orally than written, so many things have gotten lost in translation, while some things have not been transmitted at all. Then, when you factor in the burning of the library of Alexandria, you see that the majority of what we have learned as a species, and how we learned it, has been lost to the sands of time.

I point this out because if you choose to dig deeper on this subject, be careful to keep these points in mind, and view the evidence from a bias free of looking backwards, judging things by our standards.

With so many ancient structures lining up with the solstices and equinoxes, we also arrive at the conclusion that the oldest festival times worked with are these two celestial events. This becomes important later, for now it is enough to recognize this fact. Some sites even align with cosmic events, which is not even a thought today. For example, at Nabta Playa, some of the stones line up with the heliacal rising of the galactic center. When was the last time you went to a festival when an idea like this was the main purpose of the event? I have never been to one, and I have been to a lot of festivals. Following this line of thinking and applying it to mythology, the evidence we have also tells us that the goddess was much more prevalent in mass consciousness than the god, as is proven by the surviving goddess statues.

So, in a broad sense, the four oldest festival dates are the two solstices and two equinoxes, and the oldest extant deity is the goddess, not the god, as some faiths would lead you to believe. These facts also tell us that goddess traditions, especially celestial ones, are older and more potent than masculine traditions. Practically speaking, this tells us that the wheel of the year, as it is today, is closer to the truth than most belief systems.

Astromythology is the study of how myths align with the stars, not mythology that came from the stars. I offer this as a point for clarification for those that might think otherwise. I love a good ancient aliens theory as much as the next person, again it comes down to facts. Having said that, I realize that in time I might be proven wrong, and that is fine with me. I would rather have objective, undeniable proof to prove me wrong on a subject like this, than opinions rooted in subjectivity yammering in my ear like the buzzing of a bee.

The fact of the matter is, this subject has everything to do with humanity. Our species wove tales based on what they saw in the sky and how that interacted with the Earth. They were aware enough to recognize the uncommon comings and goings of events such as the solstices and equinoxes, and they took part in sacred celebrations meant to honor those auspicious times.

These ancestors also saw patterns in the stars above them and concentrated their myths on those patterns. They attached symbolism to the patterns and images that their imaginations concocted, and they wove stories about them. This happened for so long and with so many commonalities that these archetypal patterns embedded themselves in the subconscious of our species.

Recent scientific discoveries have proven what psychologists and astrologers have known for decades – that trauma can be transmitted through DNA from parent to child. It is this idea we're discussing here, only on a mass level. For more information on this, consult the writings of Dr Carl Jung. Those ancient myths have become powerful, so powerful to the degree that many consider them gods and goddesses.

Astrotheology

The third topic to briefly discuss is that of astrotheology. This is a little more complex than the other two because it is much more specific. According to Wikipedia, astrotheology is "a discipline combining the methods and domains of space science with systematic theology." That definition sounds kind of complex, so let's pick it apart. Astrotheology is the discipline (study) that combines the methods and domains (i.e., astrotheology is only discussing these topics, nothing else) of space science (a field of study that includes space exploration, natural phenomena, and physical bodies, presumably in space) with systematic theology (this will be clarified in the next paragraph).

To understand systematic theology, we must first understand theology. According to dictionary.com, theology is "the field of study and analysis that treats of God and of God's attributes and relations to the universe; study of divine things or religious truth; divinity." A secondary definition is also given: "a particular form, system, branch, or course of this study." I use two definitions here because no matter how you look at theology, it specifically and factually has to do with God, specifically the Abrahamic God and its derivatives.

According to the definition of the word, there is no such thing as a non-God oriented theology, i.e., there is no such thing as Pagan theology, or magical theology. What I say here is the strict interpretation of the word, even though there are people out there today who may beg to differ. The scientific discipline of astrotheology is therefore one hundred percent Abrahamic in nature, or at least only relegated to faiths that have a supreme God. If you believe something that does not have that, then theology will not work for you as you advance on your path.

This also means that astrotheology is not strictly scientific. If it were scientific, all references to God and other forms of religious bigotry would not be present. So, technically, contrary to popular and conservative beliefs, astrotheology is a pseudo-science.

Again, that is a conversation for another time. It is enough to know this point for now because essentially astrotheology is the study of how the stars, their cycles, space phenomenon, and space bodies, all tie into the idea of God. This makes the field quite limited because if you do not believe in God, or have no interest in blending God into science, then this might not appeal to you nor be worth checking out.

There are several examples of this, and I will discuss them here to illustrate the point.

The first one that comes to mind is the story of the Great Flood. Even though the Bible aligns this with Noah, that is not the case. In ancient Mesopotamian texts we find the same story several centuries before Judaism was created, so we know it is not a Christian story, like many people believe. Anyway, this flood lasted forty days and forty nights. Why forty? Well, when Venus retrogrades, it lasts for forty days, so we can translate this to mean that the flood lasted for the entirety of a Venus retrograde cycle in antiquity.

Some people also claim that the mythological story of the descent of the goddess Inanna into the underworld is a mythological retelling of the Venus retrograde cycle, too. You can extrapolate this out to mean that every numerical cycle you see in the Bible probably aligns with a celestial cycle. It is fun to look into that if you are interested.

Another story that comes to mind is that of the date for the celebration of the Christian holy day, Easter. The date for Easter changes every year because it is based on a formula and not a specific calendar date. The method for determining when Easter is on any given year is that it occurs on the first Sunday after the first full moon after the spring equinox of the northern hemisphere.

I clarify that it is based on the northern hemisphere's spring equinox because the spring equinox in the southern hemisphere is exactly the opposite day, so it occurs late in the calendar year. Isn't it interesting how much of the Abrahamic mythos is tied into astrology, but uneducated religious fanatics don't want you to study it?

Of the three subjects we're discussing here, this is the one that is the least impactful, even though it is probably one of the most widely known and documented.

The reason it matters the least is because it excludes spiritual traditions that do not have God, or have a Goddess in addition to a God, since the Abrahamic God's story has written out his female counterpart – Asherah.

This book is not written from a Christian perspective, so the impact of astrotheology on this text is minimal at best, if it is even present at all. I simply include it here for the sake of completion. You can take a liberal approach to astrotheology; you could broaden the definition to remove God from it so that the definition becomes 'a discipline combining the methods and domains of space science with systematic theology, regardless of the presence of God'.

The word God would still be included in the definition, although now it would be broadened to include all faiths, which is more in line with scientific thinking and true science. The etymology of the word comes from ancient Greek and breaks down as: theo (god) logy (logic). Therefore, it technically means the logic of god, and since ancient Greek was around before Christianity, we see that the original meaning of the word had nothing to do with the Abrahamic faiths. At its essence, following this line of thinking, we find that astrotheology purely means the love of the study of the gods and goddesses as they pertain to the stars and other outer space bodies and phenomenon we can perceive. This opens up the subject to real application, doesn't it?

If you pursue this line of thought, don't expect to find a lot of resources, or at least quality ones. You will find sources but most of the material out there comes from people who study this as a hobby, rather than academically trained experts. I do know several non-Christian people who have gone into theology, I also know that what they learned was predominantly Abrahamic, so while they weren't Christian, they were inundated with Christianity. This also means that they know more about that faith than most devout believers.

One of the problems you encounter when you study astrotheology is that you have to decode the wisdom it contains.

There are real pearls of wisdom to be found while studying it, however you have to remove the Abrahamic veneer to get to them, and sometimes you have to deduce what is really being shared. This can be hard work, and if you have unhealed spiritual wounds, then you may find this subject can be triggering. It took me years to work through such baggage, and I can tell you from personal experience, it is worth it to do the prerequisite healing to achieve the wisdom.

Another challenge you may encounter is that most non-Christian knowledge and wisdom has not survived the centuries thanks to the actions of religious extremists.

Specifically, I am referring to the Inquisition from the Middle Ages, as well as minor witch-hunts that occur periodically over the years. Meditation can help reveal this information, however, until it is verified through an external source, it will remain unverified, so it may be profound to you, but others might disbelieve it. You do have sources to use, such as the holy books of various faiths and sacred writings.

For example, the Norse Eddas or the Hindu Bhagavad Gita. Both contain wisdom about their deities, and with attention and education, you can extract the celestial connections.

If you can handle these challenges, you will have success adapting theology to whatever belief system you have, and in this way, liberate it from the current yoke it is under. If enough of us do this, perhaps science (specifically the soft sciences, because it is a soft science) will elevate astrotheology to where it should be, rather than where it is.

It would be wise to keep these points in mind as you work your way through the rest of this book. I offer this information here to demonstrate points, and I also want to encourage you to broaden your horizons in directions you might not look otherwise. The axle of the wheel has deep roots, and only by knowing them can you truly appreciate and adapt it to your spiritual paradigm.

CHAPTER TWO
THE MUSIC OF THE SPHERES

When learning about the ancient sacred festivals that birthed the festivals we know today, there is another thing to know which is more terrestrial in nature but is usually neglected for various reasons. Before today, the world was not as connected as it is now; telephones existed, as did newspapers, radios, and the like. With the development of the World Wide Web came a level of immediate global interconnectedness that has never occurred before. This means it is easier for people to get to know each other, and more importantly, exchange ideas that were previously isolated. As most of us have witnessed, this is both good and bad. Because of this, I feel it is time to update our perspective and knowledge. This requires refinement and study, particularly because interconnectedness seems to be the direction in which human evolution is going. Therefore, it makes sense to evolve with it, which is true spiritually as much as it is mundanely. It is this line of thought that has inspired this chapter. We can only look backward so much. There should always come a point when we start to look at the present and the future to evolve our practices as we, individually and collectively, evolve.

Even though the wheel of the year was constructed over centuries, it is important to know that there is one dominant trait usually neglected, and that is that they all come from the northern hemisphere of Earth. This does not mean that no festivals are found throughout history in the southern hemisphere, rather they have not become part of the conversation until recently, thanks to the interconnectedness we can access at will through modern technology. Hence, the wheel of the year as we know it is northern hemisphere centric. This is not bad nor good, it simply is.

The biggest reason for this is that most of the southern hemisphere is water. Far more people live in the northern hemisphere than do in the southern. And, bluntly, most of recorded human history comes from the northern hemisphere. I'm sure we all know that there is a lot of ancient history that comes from the southern hemisphere, but it is only recently that this material has started to be integrated into its proper place in our evolutionary story. From what I have learned, one of the biggest barriers is the lack of written history and records from the southern hemisphere.

This does not mean that ancient people living in the southern hemisphere could not write, or did not write, rather their records haven't survived to modern day as much as other cultures that came from the north. Throughout history, a common practice was for colonizers to burn or otherwise destroy the written words and symbolisms of the conquered people. This practice has happened due to both military conquest and ideological conquest. There have been times when a conquering religion has destroyed or stolen the information from people who were forced to convert.

Because of imperialists and religious zealots, more records of human history have been destroyed than preserved, and what has been preserved is not always translatable. There are many ancient tongues that have never been translated, and this is another factor to consider. Sometimes all it takes is to discover a key text that can help translate the material, but if no key text is found, then the information sits undeciphered, just as mysterious as ever.

Take, for example, Egyptian Hieroglyphics. Papyri and stone hieroglyphics were widely known about for centuries before the discovery of the Rosetta stone in the late 18th century that allowed translation. It is still possible we might find key texts that can help translate mysterious old languages, but with every passing day it becomes increasingly unlikely.

More of the planet is being discovered and catalogued, so there are fewer texts left to uncover to reveal secrets. Additionally, there is the human factor – sometimes humans are sitting on ancient parchments in trunks in the attics of their houses, and are unaware of the value of what they have. Sometimes, organizations, like the Vatican, hoard information because it does not support their dogma or agenda. I point out the example of the trunk in the attic because it shows that information is not necessarily hidden out of malice – sometimes it is just old-fashioned ignorance. As a person wiser than me once said, never mistake an act of ignorance for an act of maliciousness. Now that we've established why things are the way they are, let's get into the details of what this means in a practical sense, particularly how it applies to our subject.

Solstices

We're going to get technical here, so you may want to have a pen and paper handy to sketch out what I am going to explain. There are two solstices each year: one at the end of the calendar year, and one right in the middle. A solstice is when the sun reaches an extreme point as it travels across the sky during a year.

I say extreme point here, because the June solstice in the northern hemisphere is when the sun is at its highest point in the sky, so it is overhead.

During the December solstice the sun is at its lowest point in the sky, and since the sun moves across the southern sky from the northern hemisphere perspective, it is seen as being closer to the horizon. This means that the sun's influence is at its weakest, whereas in June it is at its strongest.

Remember that all of this is from a northern hemisphere perspective. This point and process is known as declination, which is used extensively in astronomy and large parts of astrology. To stimulate you further, consider this: Just like the sun has a declination, so do the planets. This is not discussed a lot, however if you look into this, you will find a wealth of information that can help fine-tune how you work with astrology, that can also bring greater detail and power into your rituals. For example, you can execute rituals when certain planets are higher in the sky than they are at other times. Or you can take note of where planets are when you do a ritual to see how that impacts your results. In some ways, you can develop this branch of study to be a very literal planetary hours system.

This is important because if we discuss the southern hemisphere and solstices, then everything is inverted. To illustrate, during the June solstice, the sun is at its highest point from a northern hemisphere perspective, but from a southern hemisphere perspective, the sun is at its weakest point in the sky, so to them, it is the winter solstice, not the summer. And conversely, the December solstice is when the sun is the strongest in the sky to them, so it is their summer solstice and the winter solstice in the northern.

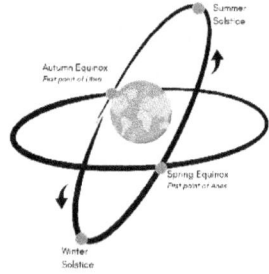

Fig 1. Diagram of ecliptic equinoxes and solstices

Equinoxes

This is an easier concept to grasp, but the inversion principle is still correct. Picture the Earth with the equator. Then, mentally or physically, draw an imaginary line out into space. This is known as the Celestial Equator.

Seasons are caused by the Earth's tilt

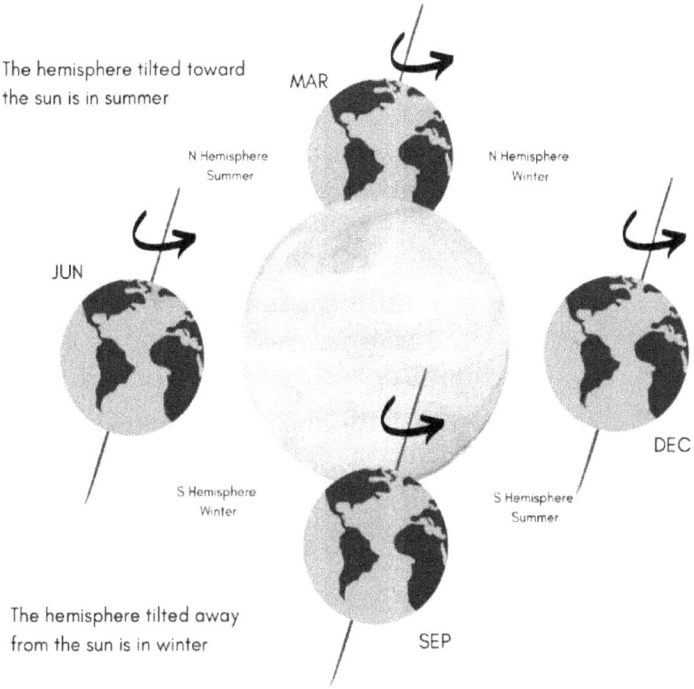

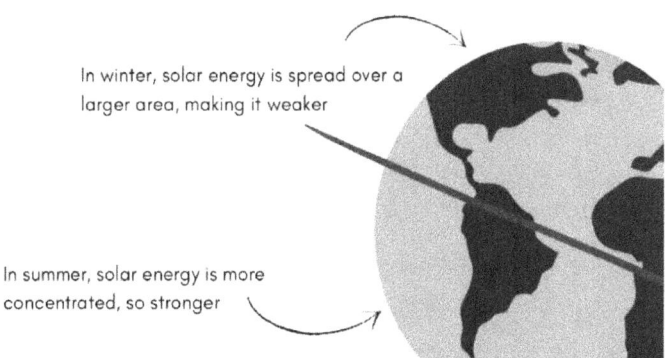

Fig 2. Diagram depicting how summer and winter differs according to the Northern and Southern hemispheres.

Twice a year the sun sits on that line, meaning that it is equal to both the northern and southern hemispheres. These are times of balancing. One equinox happens in March, and one six months later in September, just like the solstices.

In the northern hemisphere, the March equinox is considered the beginning of spring, also known as the vernal equinox, even though, as we will discuss later, this is not necessarily the case. In the southern hemisphere, this is considered the beginning of autumn, although once again, later we will discuss why this is not necessarily the case. The equinox in September is considered the autumn equinox in the northern hemisphere, in the southern it is considered the spring equinox.

*

To make an astute point, consider the following article, which demonstrates the metaphysics and rhythms behind these two points, specifically what they mean when it comes to how energy ebbs and flows.

The Metaphysics of the Veil

Excerpt from an article originally published in the *Dolmen Grove Chronicles* in Spring, 2018.

Let's start off with what we know. According to ancient Celtic and Mexican traditions, the veil between the worlds is thinnest around the time of Samhain, or the Day of the Dead. From a calendar perspective, this is around the time of October 31st through to November 2nd of each year. Other than calendar dates, this time was chosen because of changes in the natural world, and eventually became the time period we now know as Halloween. It is because of the contemporary tradition of Halloween that we know at least a little about the practices associated with this time of year.

Turning our attention to astrology, we find that all of this activity is occurring around fifteen degrees of the fixed sign of Scorpio each year. Newtonian scientific principles tell us that if something is true, so is it's opposite. The opposite of fifteen degrees Scorpio is fifteen degrees Taurus, and the festival that corresponds to that date is Walpurgisnacht / Beltane. We are then led to the fact that if the veil between the worlds is thinnest around Samhain, then it is also the thinnest around the time of Beltane.

In ancient times this was due to the fact that there were many attributes of spring that were unfolding at this time.

Further extending the logic, we find that what this also tells us is that the veil between the worlds is the thickest at the times in between these two auspicious festivals, and in this case, these are the festivals that have to do with the solstices, summer and winter. These dates vary based on where you live on the planet, but the concepts are the same.

During the summer solstice, the sun is at its highest point in the southern sky, and at the winter solstice, it is at its highest point in the northern sky. What this means is that when the sun is at its highest point in the southern sky, it is a time of maximum heat and light, and when it is at its highest in the northern sky, it is a time of maximum darkness and cold. Esoterically, we discover that the teaching given to us through this is that when extremes are present, it is the hardest to contact the plane of spirit, but I digress.

When we step back and look at the whole picture, we see a very clear system built by the natural world and available to us through our perception of this rhythm. When the veil is the thinnest, we know it is a prime time for spirit contact, and when the veil is the thickest, it is a great time to focus on subjects and ideas that have to do with the physical world and the third dimensional world that is the consensual paradigm we all share.

To fill in the gaps, let us turn our attention to Imbolc and Lughnasadh. Lughnasadh is unique because it generally coincides with the rising of the star Sirius, which played a role in many ancient cultures, ancient Egypt and the Dogon to name a couple.

However, its opposite, complimentary piece is Imbolc, which is the time of the first returning of light to the Earth. While the veil between the worlds isn't the thinnest during either of these festivals, it is worth addressing them here because the veil at both times is thinner than the solstices, but not as thin as the other two points.

The easy way to understand those two festivals is to think of it in terms of the lunar cycle. Imbolc and Lughnasadh would be considered quarter moons, and Samhain and Walpurgisnacht would be considered full moons, while the two solstices would be considered the new moons. I don't offer this information to confuse people, rather to show the best parallels I can to the energetic nature of the veil itself.

We can apply the same line of thinking and set of correspondences to the eight-spoked wheel of the year from a veil perspective that we apply to the lunar model that I just shared. The parallels between the two systems reveal to us what to expect and how to work with them in a proactive manner.

The only two points we haven't addressed yet are the equinoxes, so let us turn our attention to these. Both of these are known as periods of great balancing, so we can see these two as the time that there is a neutrality or nullification present when it comes to the veil.

Basically, at the time of the equinoxes it is wise to focus on both inner balance and balance with the outside world as well. This is a time of harmony, finding resonance with the physical world we all inhabit, and assessing what has come before and what is still to come. By evaluating where we are, we clear the mind and gain a clear perspective on our individual journeys.

We now have a fully dissected and logical view of the veil between the worlds. The interesting part about all of this information is that it doesn't conflict with any other belief system out there. Rather, it fills in the gaps for our understanding.

By understanding the rhythm and ebb and flow of the thickness between the veil, we can better plan our rituals and experiences to coincide with what is happening energetically.

When we time our work empowered with this information, we put ourselves in a position to take what would normally be average successes and turn them into larger successes.

So, for a brief recap: The veil is thinnest between the worlds at Samhain and Beltane. It is the thickest between the worlds at the solstices, and doorways of opportunities exist at the time of the equinoxes. By timing our work with these, we tap into the rhythm of the natural world to manifest greater results. There is also another detail to know, which is that during the time of the equinoxes, the magnetic field of the Earth is, on average, weaker than at other times. One of the ways this can be worked with is through the use of magnets – an underused but effective tool in magical practices. This can also be used to focus on attraction in your rituals. This includes both the law of attraction and the use of talismans. In ceremonial magick, talismans are used to attract things we want in our lives through a method other than sympathetic magick.

Why these Matter

These two points are the reason why I have arranged the chapters in the book the way I have. Allow me to explain. Let's look at the following table for clarity.

Festival	Calendar Date
Imbolc	February 1
Ostara	March Equinox
Walpurgisnacht/Beltane	April 30/May 1
Midsummer	June Solstice
Lughnasadh	August 1
Mabon	September Equinox
Samhain	October 31/November 1
Midwinter	December Solstice

Table 1. Festivals and dates of the northern hemisphere

Now, knowing what you know, you see the problem. These dates are only true in the northern hemisphere. They are not true south of the equator. South of the equator, the schedule looks like this:

Festival	Calendar Date
Lughnasadh	February 1
Autumn Equinox	March Equinox
Samhain	April 30/May 1
Winter Solstice	June Solstice
Imbolc	August 1
Spring Equinox	September Equinox
Walpurgisnacht/Beltane	October 31/November 1
Midsummer	December Solstice

Table 2. Festivals and dates of the southern hemisphere

To my knowledge, and I may be wrong, this is rarely in print. This means that as much as people like to pat each other on the back for our collective spiritual evolution, we are nowhere near as evolved as we like to think we are.

The two charts above show why I aligned the festivals the way I did in the chapters. In this book, each festival is paired with its opposite for convenience and to honor both hemispheres of the planet. In other words, a wholesome look at the wheel of the year.

In astrology it is said if you want to learn about one sign, also learn its opposite because they share traits in common. For example, if you want to learn about Samhain, then also study Beltane.

This line of thought is also true here; it is what separates this book from others on the subject – inclusiveness. Throughout this work I do my best to cater to everyone everywhere, no matter where you are on the globe. However, I do live in the northern hemisphere and everything I've read is northern hemisphere-centric, so while writing this, I am fighting against my own biases. This means that try as I might, I may well still miss a thing or two, so double check when you feel the need, and adjust accordingly. No one is perfect, after all.

This is also why it is wise to sit down at the beginning of the year and write the festivals on the appropriate days of the calendar to your area, ignoring the information you find online, especially on social media. When I make a post about a festival day, I do my best to make sure I aim it at everyone. So, when I make a statement on February 1st, not only do I say, 'Happy Imbolc,' I also say 'Happy Lughnasadh'. We're all in this together, so maybe through unity we will truly transcend.

Just because the festival dates are different, the elemental associations to the cardinal directions are not, so, regardless of where you are on the planet, air corresponds to the east, fire to the south, water to the west, and earth to the north. I have heard several conversations over the last few years that discuss changing this based on the hemisphere, but this line of thinking has not gained any traction, at least not yet, although it might in the future.

To illustrate, many years ago, a friend of mine from Australia suggested that down there, the element earth should correspond to the direction of the south, because the largest landmass closest to them is Antarctica, and since the sun is more northern in appearance, then fire should correspond to the north.

Living in the northern hemisphere, I feel I am not qualified to lead that discussion, although I do put the idea here for those that might want to explore it. Realistically, this is an area that could be profitable if you were to write books about it or even develop it as a magical system.

Because there are eight festivals throughout the year that happen regularly, common astrological phenomena also regularly occur around those times. This means we can expect things to routinely happen around the festival days. A good example of this is the eclipse cycle.

Eclipses happen in pairs, and usually there are a pair of eclipses early in the year, and a pair later in the year. The spring pair usually falls somewhere between mid-March to mid-May. Of course, there are variations on these dates, but I think you see the point. This means that you can expect eclipses around the times of the festival days that occupy that period on the calendar.

*

Another example is one that requires a little more explanation and is astrological in nature; planetary retrogrades that occur throughout the year. Although all planets retrograde, not every retrograde is the same.

A retrograde is basically an optical illusion that has to do with orbital placements and speed of the planets involved.

When a planet retrogrades, it looks like it is moving away from us and backwards to a certain extent. We know that is not the case, but that is how it appears.

Retrogrades

Excerpt from an article originally published in the *Clan Dolmen Chronicles*, Beltane, 2019.

Retrogrades are one of the more misunderstood, or at least unclarified, topics in astrology. Most of us know about them because of the Mercury retrograde periods that occur roughly three times a year, and last for three weeks at a time, but they are so much more than that. The irony is that most, if not all of us, have experienced retrogrades in one way or another throughout our lives, yet we confine this idea to just astrology. The simplest definition of the word is that it means moving backwards, or returning to a previous state, according to the *Oxford English Dictionary*. We see right there that it is not an astrologically specific term, rather it can apply to anything.

However, it is most commonly found in astrological texts and treatises, so to a casual observer, it may be seen to be astrological. One of the ways you could use this term outside of an astrological context would be when you have to roll back a piece of technology to its default factory settings. This would be retrograding it back to a previous state.

Once we put the term into an astrological context, things get a little more complex, and that is what we will focus on here. In astrology, when a planet is said to be retrograde, it is moving in a way that is contrary to its normal movement and nature. There are two examples that can clarify this, and after we look at these, we can focus on the specifically astrological nature of them.

The first example is that of going on a walk with a friend. Have you ever been on a walk somewhere and met up with a friend for a while? Of course, most people have, and I want you to visualize this in order to understand. Imagine you are walking with your friend for a while, but they go in a different direction to you. As you part ways, you look over your shoulder at your friend, and due to the direction they're walking and the direction you are walking, it may look like they are getting smaller and moving away from you, even if they are traveling in the same direction on a different trajectory. If you have had this experience, or can at least visualize what I'm saying, then you have experienced retrograde motion.

While both people are moving in the same direction, it *appears* differently, and this gives us our first insight into astrological retrograde motion. Two bodies moving at different speeds, appear to move away from each other, and optically it looks like the other is getting smaller, even though we know they are not.

This means that a large part of astrological retrograde motion is an optical trick. Basically, from our vantage point here on Earth, it looks like the planet that is retrograding is getting smaller and moving away from us, when in reality it is not. Another example that can help clarify things has to do with elementary science.

If you think back to your early childhood education, you may remember a basic scientific principle; when the Earth is closest to the sun, we have the season of summer, and when it is the farthest away from the sun, we have the season of winter. All planets in the solar system travel along their orbits at different speeds due to size and distance from the sun.

This tells us that when we are closer to the sun, or at least moving closer to the sun, the outer planets beyond Mars would be seen as retrograde from us because of their size and distance from our local star.

Conversely, this means that when we are farther away from the sun, it is the planets from Mars inward that may seem to be retrograde.

This is a rough estimate, and there are many variables to consider. If you ever find yourself in doubt, you can fall back to this line of thinking to at least have an educated guess as to whether a certain planet is retrograde or not.

See what I mean? Understanding the nature of retrograde motion is fairly easy. The tricky part is in understanding how this manifests astrologically. When a planet is retrograde, the emphasis of the qualities and properties of the planet are internally focused rather than outwardly expressed.

For example, when Mercury goes retrograde, it tells us there is something hidden beneath the surface that is calling for our attention, and it would be wise to address it, rather than complaining about it. If we don't address it, it will come back to be dealt with later, and usually in more intense ways.

The reason Mercury retrograde periods are so intense is because they are only three weeks long, and Mercury is the fastest moving planet in the solar system, so the manifestations are more dynamic. It is worth keeping this in mind because all planets in the solar system go retrograde at some point within a two-year time period, but few are as intense as Mercury.

For further illustration, let's consider this: When Saturn or Pluto go retrograde, they stay retrograde for months at a time. I use them as an example because at the time of writing this, both of them had recently gone retrograde and would remain so for quite a while. Some might read this and think that it means this will produce constant intense situations having to do with the qualities of these planets for the next several months, however nothing could be farther from the truth. Because planets are retrograde for so long, their intensity is diluted to the degree that we often forget they are retrograde.

Saturn and Pluto go retrograde every year, and this is worth keeping in mind because it removes the mental stress from us when it comes to figuring out how to deal with them. Venus and Mars only go retrograde about once every eighteen months to two years. They are so close to Earth that their orbits and speeds are similar to our own.

I hope all of this makes sense, and if you've gained a clearer understanding of retrogrades, then I have been successful.

Let's turn our attention to what to expect and how to work with this information day-to-day. There are two ways this information can be used. The first way is to pay attention to what planets are retrograde in the day-to-day sky.

By paying attention to this, we can stay on top of the subtle forces of the cosmos. The second way this information can be used is that it can bring greater clarification to our natal birth chart.

It doesn't take a lot of effort to find out what planets were retrograde when we were born. As a matter of fact, if you go to your internet search engine and type 'Swiss Ephemeris' along with the month and year you were born, a list of results will pull up. Maneuver to your birthday, and generally either an 'R' or the symbol 'Rx' will be listed on the file. When you see this, it means the planet was retrograde at the time of your birth.

In astrology, an ephemeris is your best friend, especially for things like this.

Last, and most importantly, when planets are retrograde, whether it is in your natal chart or in the changing day-to-day sky, the concept is the same.

Retrograde planets mean it is time to work on the inner life. For example, if you have Mars retrograde in your natal chart, it means this is a time to work internally with all of the qualities of Mars, which includes working positively with masculine energy, energy management in all of its forms, motivation for your ambitions, and the essence of energy itself – prana. When a planet is retrograde in the sky on any given day, the same rule applies, but generally events happen in the outside world that bring our attention to the work that needs to be done, internally speaking.

Even though I give you the basics of retrogrades here, I will not list each planet and their retrograde meanings – how this material manifests in your chart and in your life is highly subjective to your individual chart, so there is almost no way I could discuss every single feature. Suffice to say, if you want to immediately start working with this information, look up the planet you want to start with and consider the correspondences and what that would mean for you from an internal perspective. Like reversed tarot cards, retrogrades address the inner life rather than the external one, and because of this, it takes a shift in consciousness and behavior to really, truly work with them for your own greatest growth and good.

Now, I hope this makes more sense than what you might see on random, fandom websites. It can be confusing and daunting out there in the World Wide Web in general, and this is especially true when it comes to this subject.

One final piece of information to consider is that generally the average person has three planets or more in retrograde in their natal chart, and the more retrograde planets, the more this is a lifetime in which it is wise to focus on internal development. Conversely, if you have no retrograde planets in your birth chart, or next to none, then this is a lifetime of forward momentum and forward progress, rather than a lot of internal self-reflection and healing. Enjoy this excursion into personal development.

*

You can see from the two articles reprinted above that they were released a year apart, and there is some crossover even though they focus on different topics. In the following chapters I will be reprinting articles that correspond to the time of the year that aligns with a particular festival season to give you an idea of what to energetically expect each year, and while dates may vary, they will not vary by much. This is how you bring your festival work alive.

By knowing what to look for energetically, you can more finely tune your work to tap into subtleties and nuances others may miss, thereby producing larger than expected results. You may even surprise those around you with your almost prophetic ability to know what's happening astrologically without following astrological placements religiously. Below is another article that illustrates a regular feature to look at especially towards the beginning of the year.

This article stresses the importance of looking ahead at the year when it comes to astrology, and how it might impact your personal and public work. Is there a Mercury retrograde happening around the time of a public get together? If so, you might want to make a plan B, or allow extra time when dealing with it. If there is no festival present, then you can use this look ahead to help you deal with other life issues that might be prevalent at the time. That's the nice thing about astrology – everything is rhythms and patterns, and when you learn to identify them, you can put them to work for you when planning rituals, life events and choices.

State of Affairs

Excerpt from an article originally published in the *Dolmen Grove Chronicles* in Spring, 2019.

Some of you may have noticed that there is a lot of motion in the stars right now, and that is being reflected across the globe with a lot of upheavals and changes happening in a variety of countries and areas around the planet. While these events may seem intense, I can assure you that things are only going to get more intense over the next several years. However, before we get into that discussion, let's turn our attention to the present moment.

When equinox rolls around, we have an interesting astrological situation. First of all, there is a Mercury retrograde occurring, which tells us a major theme until mid-April is that of resolving emotional and spiritual situations that may have caused a lot of inner turmoil and headaches in the recent past.

While this is an ongoing situation for most people, the astrology of the moment tells us things are more intense than normal, and more widespread. Adding further credence to this is the fact that we have a sun-Chiron conjunction in Aries.

Chiron is the planet of the wounded healer, and when it is conjunct the sun it tells us the wounds being addressed are ones that have to do with an overall sense of self. Feelings of low self-value, self-worth, self-confidence, and self-esteem, among other things, are what are being addressed when you read between the lines. The problem is that not everyone addresses these exposed wounds in the same way. Some recoil in fear, or hide behind horrible behavior, while others take the opportunity to do some introspection and self-reflection to promote healing.

In addition to all of this emphasis on wounds and healing, we also have Uranus moving into Taurus. It has been wavering back and forth between Aries and Taurus for quite some time, and now we find it firmly rooted in the sign of the bull. Uranus is the planet of the internet, electricity, eccentricity, individuality, and rebellion. Taurus is an earth sign, and is the most condensed of all, meaning that it is as earthy as it can get.

So, when we put the two together, we see that the seven-year period that is coming up is all about expressing your uniqueness and individuality on the physical plane. Besides this, when it comes to society, there may be common rebellions, either on a social level or a personal level.

Working with the physical world, society, the planet, and all things related to physical manifestation is going to be a major theme over the next six years, as we move through a Pluto-Saturn conjunction in Capricorn, which is another earth sign. Coming up over the next several years it is time, individually and collectively, for all of us to focus on the physical planet, moving through society, and integrate with the world around us.

The time of transformation is at hand, but it's not the spiritual aspects of this that are being emphasized, rather, the physical manifestation of change. No longer is it wise to retreat into a shell to avoid the outside world. Now is the time to become integrated in the world around us to be the change you wish to see, to borrow a phrase. I'm not going to get into any sort of debate or discussion on climate change, however, I do want to point out that the poles of the planet are shifting; ice is melting in great quantities, and the planet is changing in ways we are still studying.

Perspectives aside, we can look at this time period as one of profound change, and historically speaking, a lot of this is right on schedule. However, the other factor involved here is the influence of humanity on this planet, and what it has done, for better or worse.

This is worth noting because there are some things we can't change, such as the poles shifting, but there are some things we can change, such as our use of fossil fuels, pollution, and the way we treat the planet. In addition to the element of earth being prominent at this time, water is playing a major role as well.

Earlier in this piece I focused on the emotional and spiritual side of the equation, but there is something different at play here in a subtler way. This is the spiritual initiation that is currently occurring and will be developing over the next several years. Water is the element associated with spiritual initiation, and all one has to do is look around to see how this is playing out on the grand stage.

Organized religions are going through a major overhaul, as there is a dichotomy between increased attendance in extremist faiths and denominations, yet an increasing number of people who are not of that mindset are leaving organized religion. Scandals are becoming more common, and most involve basic human rights.

There is a growing intolerance of subhuman behavior, especially as it pertains to racism, sexism, and most '-isms' out there.

People are no longer being quiet about injustices, and many are becoming proactive when it comes to making changes.

There is a problem with this though, all of the things that are being challenged are long-standing institutions, ingrained thought patterns of the species, and generational teachings that have been passed down from one generation to the next. As we see, not everyone is on board with the change that is occurring.
While this does tie in to what I mentioned above about people being resistant to change, this is also different because there is a lot of change happening very, very quickly. It can be challenging enough for some people to embrace a small amount of change but requiring generations of people to change most of their world view in a short amount of time is a lot to ask.

Resistance to change is understandable and this is worth keeping in mind when dealing with people who are not adapting at a rate we may desire. By keeping this in mind, we keep our humanity, compassion, and empathy close to our hearts. The human species has always walked a fine line between being very emotional and very analytical, and this is the age-old battle between the animal mind and the human mind. After all, we should never forget we are animals.

I realize this may sound like a tangent but it is all part of the spiritual initiation we are undergoing as a species. Maintaining compassion in the face of those who do not share our views is becoming a very valuable skill. Another valuable skill is that of spiritual discernment. Becoming upset at things that are out of our control is not very wise in the first place and in this age of information overload, it is easy to lose sight of where to draw the line.

The tradeoff to this is that more and more things are under our control because it is increasingly easier to network and coordinate with people across the planet that may share our views. Thus, the line becomes blurred and sometimes difficult to manage.

Seeing with increased clarity is a major skill to develop this year and going forward. I have seen some people on the internet discuss the fact that next year is 2020, and therefore can be seen as a time of clarifying vision. There is some truth to this, and it would be wise to keep the idea of clarity in all forms in mind as we approach next year.

The theme of this year is wrapping up things that have been unresolved, for quite some time now.

Next year we move into a different space – the space of new beginnings and seeing things as they are rather than how we want to see them.

Long-time practitioners will see that this is a huge departure from approximately the last fifty years of spiritual emphasis and movement.

For the last fifty years the emphasis has been on elevating the consciousness of the species, and most of this has had to do with manipulating the finer energies of the cosmos. Now we find ourselves in a position to take what we have learned and bring it down to physical results.

The difference between now and then is that an engagement in society and the greater world is more prominent and encouraged than in previous decades.

So, where does this leave us?

Basic metaphysics, of course. In the order of the planes, water is one step above and removed from the physical.

This tells us the more emotionally invested we get in enacting physical changes over the next seven years or so, the more progress and success we can achieve.

We can't get too attached to those emotions, as there is such a thing as too much.

For the moment, it would be wise to focus on what needs to be resolved and healed, and when this is accomplished to the best of your ability, turn your attention to how to implement, in very physical ways, new, improved behaviors, structures, and social changes that are in line with living in harmony with the planet, and our fellow humans.

*

Below is another article that illustrates what has and can happen during these times, particularly solstices.

To identify a season as inspirational, or creative, or another other adjective you prefer, does require a slightly deeper application of astrology than just knowing sun signs and basic information, so be warned that if you want to work with the ideas in the following article, you may find you have to sharpen up your astrology skills.

A Season of Inspiration

Excerpt from an article originally published in the *Dolmen Grove Chronicles* in summer, 2021.

On June twentieth, we have the solstice. I refrain from calling it the summer solstice because that is only correct for the northern hemisphere. In the southern, it is the winter solstice.

Regardless of where you are, there is one constant found during this time, and that is the constant of inspiration. Let's take a closer look at the upcoming season to see what I mean.

First, how good are you at seeing your own areas for improvement? The solstice in June begins while Mercury is retrograde, which means it is the perfect time to identify the problems that come up in life because those are areas of the self that need addressing.

All this requires is humility and understanding, so it takes minimal effort. Step one is to identify what needs work and why. Following this is where things get interesting because we move from self-reflection to contacting the great beyond.

What makes this accurate at this time is that Jupiter is currently stationing. Stationing is when a planet is in the middle of shifting from retrograde motion to direct motion, or direct motion to retrograde motion. In this case, Jupiter is stationing from being direct to retrograde. The length of a stationing period is determined by the planet – specifically, the speed of the planet, which is also put into context of the speed of Earth – and the orbit taken around the sun. Mercury only stations for about twelve hours at a time, whereas outer planets like Jupiter take days.

Astrologically, the stationing period can manifest as 'anything goes' because the stationing planet is doing something different from what it usually does, but that difference is not in line with retrograde or direct behavior. Sometimes this manifests as occasional quirks or glitches in the affairs of said planet.

I remember one time about ten years ago that Saturn was stationing for several days, and during that time, the air just felt heavy, and things took a lot longer to accomplish than they normally did. These were byproducts of Saturn-time, heaviness, a feeling of lead instead of gold.

When Jupiter is stationing, it means that there may be something fishy going on with your finances, and it could also mean that the energy is more conducive to spirit contact than other times. This is especially the case now, as we will see as we break this down.

When Mercury is retrograde, it generally makes it easier to meditate and go within for guidance and wisdom. A few days after the solstice, Mercury retrograde blends with the north node of the moon in Gemini, which tells us that it is a prime time to figure out where to go from here, spiritually speaking. One of the better ways to accomplish this is through personal communication, whether the other person is in spirit or flesh.

When Jupiter is stationing, the same effect might manifest. If those two indicators are not enough, we also have that season in June starting with four planets in water signs, and water signs are known as being intuitively or spiritually focused. These three factors all tell us that this will be the perfect time to develop your spirit contact.

These also tell us this is an excellent time to seek guidance from the finer planes or external spiritual beings around us who support us.

Water signs also generally correspond to spiritual initiation, so if you have been looking for a good time for that kind of activity, it would be a good time during these three months.

Water signs also correspond to emotions, so if you're not careful, you might get dragged into creating drama, intentionally or not, or you may be surrounded by people that create drama to feed off of it, like the toxic vampires that they are, even if it is unintentional. Saturn also spends a good portion of that season in retrograde, meaning it is an excellent time to review how you do things and see if there is a better way that is now available to you that wasn't before.

All of the water sign activity also brings our creativity to the forefront of life. This makes it a good time to start a new hobby or other creative endeavor. There are many benefits to this. Firstly, whatever you develop can be an excellent vessel for self-expression. Secondly, having a creative habit like this can also be a good way to blow off steam if stress levels get too high. Embracing and developing your creativity can also be great to open the mind to new and different ways to contact spiritual beings. One of the things I enjoyed from my time as a musician is the trance nature of playing the instrument. When the groove is right, you can get lost in it for hours, and with discipline and training, that can be an excellent channel for information and beings to come through.

Cynics in the room may think that these opportunities are around us all the time, so noting them now is not so special, and while that is the case on a small scale, that criticism falls apart on a bigger scale. By the time the equinox in September rolls around, the emphasis drastically changes to that of internal reflection and changes, due in part to the fact that most of the water sign emphasis has faded and is replaced with air, making it a good time for reasoned plans and the use of logic, and not spiritual initiation or powerful insights. Certain individuals may still experience profound initiations and insights then, which is due to the nature of their astrological charts. Still, by and large, that will not be the case for most people, whereas, in the upcoming season, it will be true more so than not.

We are not necessarily aware of the initiations that we go through in life. Many people don't realize that your first job is an initiation, or when you work for yourself instead of someone else is an initiation, too. Sometimes we only see the initiation in the rear-view mirror of our self-reflection. Make this season yours. This is what it is for this year.

If you have been planning on moving ahead with any of these themes, this will be the time to do it. Suppose you do not plan on doing anything like this. In that case, that is fine, too, because the Mercury retrograde will bring things to your attention to address anyway, meaning you will get further initiated into the mysteries of Mercury, the patron of tricksters, thieves, swindlers, communication, and alchemy. Do you want to test those odds?

*

I hope these articles give you enough information to work with, and also inspire you to challenge how you view the world. What words do you use to describe various seasons of your life? How about aligning your decisions and activities with what is happening astrologically? Sometimes the biggest hurdle we face is not being able to give words to experiences, and if we cannot label something, we cannot control it, and we have a hard time processing it.

CHAPTER THREE
THE BASELINE

The next few articles all have the common theme of giving an overview of the last few years. I share them, knowing that they are dated, to give you an idea of how to use astrology at the beginning of the calendar year to look ahead for the sake of planning.

Patterns are everywhere in astrology, and this makes our work easier. For example, in the teens of this century, a common astrological pattern was that Mercury was always retrograde at the beginning of the year. So, when you saw that pattern, you figured out what to expect and how to adapt to the upcoming year to start off on the right foot.

Now, a different pattern is in place at the beginning of the calendar year; there will be a block of time spanning several months near the first of the year when the significant planets looked at in astrology are direct all at once. This gives you a green light from the universe to move ahead with new projects for the coming year.

This does mean you have to stay on top of it when it comes to paying attention, astrologically speaking, but you don't have to do a deep dive. There are many ways you can use this to your advantage spiritually and mundanely, so let your imagination and ambition be your guides.

For example, if you have been wanting to start a magical group, this can prove invaluable. Or, if you have been looking for a sign to move ahead with a work-related project, you can use this insight to help you with that. Of course, the other alternative is to consult an astrologer, we are easy to find, especially on the internet. Of course do your background check, too. The biggest challenge you may face is finding someone as equally versed in astrology as they are in occultism.

These articles also establish a baseline for where we are at now, astrologically speaking. They were written at the beginning of the decade and therefore give us insight into why and how things are now. We're almost halfway through the decade, so we are realistically halfway through the neo-Roarin' Twenties. A lot has changed since these articles were written, but some things that happened then are still rippling out now.

The first article came out in 2019, so I realize that is technically part of this decade, however considering everything that has happened since then, it feels pertinent to add it.

The Coming Age

Excerpt from an article originally published in the *Clan Dolmen Chronicles* in the New Year issue, 2019.

There is an overused phrase, nay, a concept, that a lot of people are tired of hearing, but it is truer now than it has been before. The concept is that of living in an especially important age. Variations include, 'You're living in the most critical of times', or 'This time period is the most important of your life'. I won't get into all of the other variations on this theme, as I am confident you know what I mean. This idea that where we are now is so much more important than other time periods is one that is commonly found in many places, ranging from nihilistic Christian beliefs that these are the end times to the other end of the spectrum, the New Agers (whatever that means!) who say this is one of the most profound periods of time to be alive. There is a whole spectrum in between these two points, and I'm sure you're tired of hearing it, too.

So, if I know you're tired of hearing it, why am I bringing it up? That, my friends, will be the focus of this article. Astrologically speaking, we ARE living in profound times, but maybe not for the reasons you may think.

Let's back up a moment to the latter part of 2011/2012. This was the time that there was a lot of emphasis on the end of the Mayan calendar and what that could mean. There was a lot of hype in the air about that date, and of course there was a backlash to it, too. To begin with it was the end of the Mayan calendar, but on December 31st every year it's the end of the current calendar, too, so why should the Mayan calendar be anything more special than that?

Just because it was the last writings of the Mayan timekeepers doesn't mean it would be the end of anything special. It just means that is where they quit writing things down. And, considering that their culture seemingly vanished overnight, it makes sense they would stop writing down their calendars, too. Of course, the people didn't disappear overnight, but that's a different story.

It is worth noting that in a lot of ways the Mayan calendar was more accurate than the calendar we still use to this day.

After all, astrology, and most western timekeeping tools such as calendars and clocks are based on cycles of twelve, which corresponds to Jupiter, and there is a direct correlation there. However, the Mayan calendar was based on cycles of two, more specifically, cycles of Venus. I don't know about you, but I find it easier to remember things from two months ago rather than things from twelve months ago!

While trite, this does serve as the underlying lesson. During the height of the use of this calendar, the transmission of information was a lot more basic than it is today. There were no hard drives, no cellular phones. There were sticks, stone, and rock. We can see that it is easier to record and transmit information over a two-year period than twelve years, and it is because of this that the Mayan calendar is more accurate. The end of the Mayan calendar told us that a particular age was coming to a close, nothing more, and nothing less.

At the time of 2012 I was working in a metaphysical shop, and had been for a number of years, and I can tell you from firsthand experience that since December 21, 2012, sales of sage, common here in the USA for energetic cleansing, have gone through the roof.

The Vatican has discussed quite frequently that the number of possessions and exorcisms have increased since then as well. All of this information tells us that since that point, the veil between the worlds is thinner than previously, and that more and more people are addressing these things when they come up, rather than ignoring them or trying to rationalize in unhealthy ways, so that they don't face that half of existence. What this means is that we are now in a more spiritual age.

When I say spiritual here, I simply mean of the spirit world, and not that misunderstood concept of someone who focuses on their personal development and tries to call that spirituality. Spirituality has to do with interacting with spirits and the spirit world. We can see that now the veil is thinner, and people are also more attentive to these things. This is one proof of the age we are in, and the age that is coming up.

For those of you who might be curious, I'm not going to touch on the Age of Aquarius position. In short, we're not there yet but we are in the shadow of it coming into being. To know more about this, study the works of the Irish astrologer, Cyril Fagan, for he explains it mathematically. You could throw this into the mix too, just for fun.

The next point, which is a lot more applicable, is the Pluto return of the USA. Pluto takes approximately 248 years to go through the zodiac back to where it was at the time of birth. This is called a Pluto return. Therefore, people don't have Pluto returns but nations do. In astrology, Pluto is the planet of deep-rooted transformation and change. It is the planet of diving down deep, confronting darkness, finding hidden wealth, and being changed for it. However, Pluto is also the planet of violence, abuse, and accidents.

A good example of a Pluto return was the French revolution. This occurred at the Pluto return of France and we see how that went. The impoverished of France saw the abuses, greed, corruption, and gluttony of those in power and took matters into their own hands with the drop of a blade. The Pluto return of the USA is coming up very, very soon, and we are arguably in its shadow period already.

How will this play out for the USA? That's a good question, and if you ask six astrologers, you might get eighteen different answers. No-one knows for sure, but there are some hints and clues we can look at as indicators. The first situation is that of racism and white power. Even though there was just a civil war fought about this, it is still alive and kicking.

Systemic discrimination is still present, as is sexism. Another growing indicator is the increased gap between the Haves and Have Nots. Echoing the French revolution, there is a growing divide between the poor and the rich. Themes of sexuality and the abuses thereof are also present, as are themes of sexual repression, especially that espoused by religion. Oh, and yeah, religion and the problems that come with it are front and center here in the USA as well. And let's not forget the medical crisis, either.

Just with these few themes we have cultivated a rich garden for the seeds of destruction to bloom.

Some might say that they are glad this is confined to one country, and people may especially say that if they don't live in the USA, and I do completely understand.

However, with the USA, you have something slightly different in that what occurs in the USA will ripple out across the rest of the planet to a certain degree, leaving almost no one unaffected. There is strong potential that global changes and impacts may be brought on as a result of what is happening.

Interestingly enough, at the time of this writing, there are protests in France over low wages for workers, among other social ills, and in the USA, there is quite the disconnect in general, and it is a large enough of a country that this applies in many different ways to many different people.

The dates for the height of intensity for the USA Pluto return is approximately 2020 to 2025. As we all know, social unrest isn't confined to specific years like a cat in a box, and thus things are already coming into being, and the fallout will most likely last longer than just 2025.

When you step back and look at the whole picture as I lay it out here, it is easy to see that we are living in profound times, however this has nothing to do with the end of days prayed for by Christians, nor the nebulous prophecies of dissatisfied people. These are interesting times because a decade from now the landscape of the world, specifically as it has to do with society and people, may be vastly different than it is today.

Then again, the only constant is change.

2020, Year of Clarity

Excerpt from an article originally published in the *Dolmen Grove Chronicles* in 2019.

To those of you who have been faithful readers of my material in this column, and in other places on the internet, this article will get into more detail for the upcoming period of intensity. For years I, and many other astrologers, have been discussing what is coming up between 2020 and 2025, and we get a wakeup call on January 10th or 11th, depending on where on the globe that you live. So, let's turn our attention to what kicks it all off: this eclipse.

Okay, so really, while this is the first eclipse of the year, it is actually the second in a pair of eclipses that begins in December of 2019. In that way, it will readdress themes that came to light then.

There's also the reminder that even though this is the first eclipse of the calendar year, it is not the first of the zodiacal year. It is the second in the pair that kicks off in late December. In a lot of ways, we get a sneak peek into what to expect by looking at the eclipse that just happened in the middle of July 2019.

You could extrapolate this to say that in order to understand the eclipses of December 2019 and January 2020, it would be wise to look at the pair of eclipses that just occurred in July, as the two pairs of eclipses are largely mirrors of each other. What this means is that the upcoming eclipses will manifest in inverse ways. For example, the eclipses in July mostly had to do with themes of security and the immediate family, but the upcoming pair will largely have to do with the occupation, career, and overall direction of life.

Capricorn is the opposite sign of Cancer, and the upcoming eclipses are happening in Capricorn, whereas the two in July were in Cancer. Capricorn is the sign of the occupation, career, overall direction of life, and also the sign of traditional structures and institutions. Since Pluto began moving through Capricorn in 2008, the transformation (Pluto) of traditional structures in society (Capricorn) has been a reoccurring theme, and we are only now building towards the climax, occurring over the next five years or so.

There will be more than just this eclipse in 2020 as there is a lot happening through the whole year, and if we look at this particular event we will get a sense of what to expect. So, let's break it down.

The first thing to note is that a major theme will be on the harmony and balance between the immediate family and home life, in contrast to the occupation, career, and necessary changes in otherwise traditional social structures. All of this is influenced by a spiritual change that is occurring as Neptune continues to move through Pisces. Neptune has been here for quite some time, so the changes have been subtle, and when we look back, we can see its influence.

In many countries over the globe, religion and spirituality are becoming predominant themes. In a lot of these places, it is a contrast of extremism, as there is a lot of conflict currently between extremism, moderation, and pioneering.

However, in some places, such as the USA, finer things get to come to the surface as well. The best example of this is The Satanic Temple. Advocates of social and political causes focused on religious equality, they have made major inroads to help level the playing field, so to speak. Coupled with the fact that adherence to traditional religious structures is diminishing almost monthly, it paints quite the picture of the spiritual changes that are occurring in the nation.

These are all indicative of the Neptune transit, and while we use the USA as an example here, it is safe and reasonable to conclude that similar envelope-pushing discussions are happening in various other nations across the planet. What we experience in January will be necessary changes conducive to the spiritual growth and development of the species overall. This doesn't necessarily mean we'll be able to make sense of it now, as often times we have a hard time seeing what is really happening until we are through it.

Also of note is that all of the main planets in astrology will be direct. This means that it will be a time of moving ahead and that will be the energy that starts the year. There are a couple of exceptions to this, just so we're clear. The first is that the north node of the moon is retrograde, it is for approximately 95% of the year, so the gravity it brings to the situation can be mitigated to next to nothing.

The other exception is that technically, Uranus is not direct, as it is stationing. Stationing is when a planet is in between being retrograde or direct, and the time period for this varies on the planet being discussed. With Uranus, this period is generally several days, whereas with Mercury it is only a few hours.

Uranus is the planet of the internet, mass communication, electricity, rebellion, eccentricity, individuality, and uniqueness, to name only a few correspondences. Thus, when Uranus is stationing, it tells us that 2020 will be a year of the unexpected, and probably manifesting in extreme ways, due to what we discussed about Capricorn, and in social ways, for the same Capricorn reason.

To better narrow down our timing, it is wise to look at Mars, because Mars provides the energy. Mars moves into Capricorn riding roughshod over the planets already there several weeks after the eclipse, and it isn't until March that it makes contact with the heavy hitters of Jupiter, Saturn, and Pluto, thus, it isn't until March that things really pop off. What we confront in January will be part of two things that came into being in July 2019, tying off those two ends of time.

Between now and January, it would be wise to review what has happened since July in order to gauge where your life will be most impacted between January and March of next year, the year of clarity.

2020 Eclipses and Moons

Excerpt from an article originally published in the *Dolmen Grove Chronicles* in 2019.

"Those who would give up essential Liberty, to purchase a little temporary Safety, deserve neither Liberty nor Safety." ~Benjamin Franklin

In the previous article, we took a look at what the year 2020 will bring us in a broad context. Now we will focus on some of the details, specifically the lunar phases of the year, the full moon in early January, and the final eclipse of the year in December. Remember that lunar phases, new and full, between now and then, will be steps of progress from the first one in January until the final one in December.

The easy way to look at this is to see that the lunar cycle for 2020 ends with the new moon in December, and the final full moon being the launch pad for 2021.

The lunar eclipse on January 10th brings an extreme emphasis on two signs, Capricorn and Cancer. This highlights the themes that will be addressed for the first several weeks of 2020. Capricorn is the sign of the father, long-standing institutions, doing things alone, responsibilities, maturity, and the career.

Conversely, Cancer is the sign of the mother, nurturing, the home and all things related to it, your roots, and security.

The weight of the eclipse favors Capricorn energy, but the Cancer energy is worth noting too, because it forms a tense opposition to all that activity. Hence, on the surface, we find the struggle between developing security and charging boldly ahead in one's life. The secret to achieving success is to find the balance between the two, and to avoid the psychological pitfall of choosing one over the other. I mention this last point here because we are currently divided in a lot of ways in a lot of countries, with the two extremes being Haves and Have Nots; liberalism versus conservatism.

Being polarized is something that all of us see when we look at the media and what is going on in the world around us. We are currently divided as a species, which has been well discussed in other outlets, and it is this eclipse that will heighten that division and tension. Thus, overall themes focus on moving ahead versus focusing on security.

Some people may retreat into seeking comfort over growth, while others may move forward so much that they don't follow safe practices.

On a personal note, you may find that January focuses on bringing internal issues to the surface, and in this way, it may require you to face your internal fears and prejudices in order to move ahead for your greatest growth and good. This eclipse is happening in the south node of the moon, meaning that this is a time of release. Thus, this is the beginning of the year's journey.

The rest of the lunar phases, new and full, over the course of the year, are ones that are based around the theme of exploration, both of the self and of others. While each lunar phase will bring with it its own themes, the prevailing theme of all of them has to do with searching for solutions for issues being dealt with and ways to move forward productively. The other part of the equation lies in finding your spiritual path for the next leg of the journey. Part of this entails freedom and directness, and it also addresses having courage, in particular the courage of your convictions.

During the unfolding of the year, if you want more information on these themes, investigate the nodes of the moon in Gemini and Sagittarius. The nodes of the moon represent where we are growing, spiritually speaking, and in this context, it would refer to the growth of the species as a whole.

The nodes also represent where we've come from, spiritually speaking – in this case, where we have been – and also what we are most comfortable with.

During the January eclipse, the north node of the moon (where we're spiritually going) is in Cancer, and the south is in Capricorn (where we have come from). This is why that eclipse is so strong. It is literally telling us to decide how to proceed and how important it is to have courage and move ahead. Soon after this eclipse, the nodes move into Gemini from Cancer, and Sagittarius from Capricorn. Gemini is a curious sign, and Sagittarius is the sign of spirituality and travel. Therefore, the spiritual themes of the year have to do with curiosity in the name of developing spirituality, and at the same time not getting stuck in the search for variety, ultimately coming down to one singular decision and path forward.

When the solar eclipse of December 14, 2020 arrives, the journey of the year comes to a close. The tension and struggle between the two polar opposites has run its course. In a lot of ways, this is a time of choice on how to proceed. You've had all year to explore and experience, and it is time to make a decision in line with who you are now, rather than who you were when you first formulated your initial spiritual beliefs.

Since this is a new moon, the energy will not be as tense as it was in January and may even manifest as liberating. Beware that there may still be a pull towards your comfort zone and leaving it may take an act of courage. It is through this courage that liberation and transformation can be achieved.

This sets the stage for 2021, when you may find freedom and spiritual growth through its expression, the main themes both personally and collectively.

This fiery energy can propel you forward into 2021 more on your terms than has been common over the last few years. Remember that all of this is building up to play out until 2026, so while optimism may be the theme at the beginning of 2021, it should be kept in check and used as motivation and fuel, and not as an end in itself.

*

We'll move on to 2021 with the next article, which discusses a rare astrological event called a Great Conjunction that occurred that year. As a matter of fact, you know what this is, you just don't realize that you know it.

The Great Conjunction of 2021

Excerpt from an article originally published in the *Clan Dolmen Chronicles* in the New Year's issue, 2021.

The title of this piece is a little deceptive but applicable for all of 2021, so allow me to explain. We have a rare astronomical and astrological alignment in late December of 2020 that is in full effect for 2021 until about the same time the following year. This is the conjunction of Jupiter and Saturn in Aquarius. A conjunction between these two planets happens roughly every twenty years, in different astrological signs each time. When Jupiter and Saturn are conjunct, it is known as the Great Conjunction because of these two planets' size. Both of these are known as social planets in astrology, and together they show how the individual connects with society at large.

Jupiter is the planet of prosperity, expansion, good fortune, teaching, rulership, and spirituality. Traditionally, it corresponds to the gods that rule pantheons. To use a Thelemic concept, Jupiter is Nuit. Saturn is just the opposite. In astrology, Saturn is the planet of contraction, foundation, lessons, stability, time, karma, boundaries, and death.

Generally, it corresponds to death deities in various pantheons. Thelemically, it is Hadit. I use the two Thelemic examples because they are both accurate with how they apply to the planets and how the planets apply to each other. Jupiter is the exhale of breath, and Saturn is the inhale.

This conjunction is exceptional because this is the closest conjunction between them as they relate to Earth since the year 1623. Not much of particular note happened that year, so this conjunction does not mean anything exceptional in that regard. The last time these two planets were in Aquarius was the year 1405, and the only things of particular note were the Chinese setting sail to explore the world and the Mongol empire collapsing.

There is a technique you can use in astrology to do some forecasting with this conjunction. You cast a chart for the time of the exact conjunction, and that can be used to see how things are going to go until the next conjunction. So basically, it gives you a look into the next twenty years, with regards to humanity's interaction with each other, and to themselves.

This is a narrow lens for forecasting and I won't expand on it here. I want you to know you can play around with this if you desire.

From a spiritual and religious perspective, there is a story I would like to share here, which is worth pondering and can give us some insight into what to expect in a broad sense.

In 1603, the scientist, Johannes Kepler, believed that the fabled Star of Bethlehem was a conjunction between Jupiter and Saturn. Thus, Jesus the Christ was born with this conjunction in his chart (if he existed). In his work, he calculated a triple conjunction between Jupiter, Saturn, and the sun. It should be noted that this triple conjunction is not a conjunction of three celestial bodies, as would logically be the case, rather in his scenario, this was the conjunction of Jupiter and Saturn in opposition to the sun.

While doing his research, he arrived at 7 BCE, which is a far cry from the suspected birth date of Jesus in 32 BCE. Using a computer and software, I took a look at what he was looking at, and things lined up differently to the connections he made. The date of 7 BCE was the same, but the date was December 5th, 7 BCE, not December 25th. Most of us know that Jesus was not born on December 25th in any year, so this is not surprising.

This conjunction was in Pisces, not Aquarius, which does fit the narrative of the Piscean age.

In that way, you could say that this upcoming conjunction may be another step forward towards the Age of Aquarius, which is continually unfolding around us, even though we are not quite there yet.

It is suspected that John the Baptist (if he lived) was born under this conjunction, rather than Jesus the Christ, which does conflict with Kepler's thesis. So, I decided to go back to the previous Great Conjunction before that, which occurred in 26 BCE, on June 29th, in the fixed fire sign of Leo. This is much closer to the rumored birth of Jesus, so this could fit. And the conjunction before that would be approximately twenty years earlier, so it would be around 46 BCE, specifically October 6th, 46 BCE. The sign it was in was the fixed water sign of Scorpio. This is a possibility for the actual year of the birth of Jesus the Christ, even though it would put his age as older than Christianity says he was when he died.

The findings of my research have been lackluster and disappointing. Suppose you look at all of the dates mentioned from a historical perspective. In that case, there are very few common themes that run between them, so it is difficult to say that a particular event will happen during this conjunction.

Since this conjunction happens every twenty years, there are frequent historical events that happen during them. Still, I focus on the dates in this article to explore the religious and spiritual side of things. It looks like Kepler could have been on to something with his thesis, however the dates I get don't line up with his, although the concepts are aligned. The last time this particular conjunction happened in Aquarius was the fall of the Mongol Empire and China's exploration across the greater ocean, so if history does repeat itself in some way, we may see the fall of empire(s), as well as the beginning of an exploration into the greater unknown. Like most things, in my opinion, this will be determined by the free will of the people involved in such things, as is always the case.

Magically, this conjunction is occurring on winter solstice in the northern hemisphere and summer solstice in the southern. Aquarius is the sign of community, group activities, science, logic, reason, doing what is best for all involved, and universal brotherhood. It is the 5th Ray in the Seven Rays system in Theosophy and aligns with the Ascended Master Hilarion. Working together for the betterment of all summarizes Aquarian energy.

The winter solstice is the time of the longest night, absolute darkness, and cold, and simultaneously, the time of the immediate family and close friends. The hearth is an image that summarizes this energy.

The summer solstice is that time of enjoying the sun's warmth, manifestation, creativity, heat, and the longest day. You can see that the overall theme is that of community, oneness, exploration, science, logic, and reason. Where you are in the world helps you decide how you want to tap into this energy.

Finally, even though this conjunction occurs in December of 2020, it will last all through 2021. This is due to how slow the two planets move and when factoring in their retrograde periods. It technically doesn't end until mid-December 2021, so this conjunction of energy and emphasis on groups and doing what is best will be with us through the entire year next year.

It would be quite easy to execute a ritual on the solstice to capture and align with this energy and then work with it next year. After all, all of us are together on this big rock, hurtling through space.

*

I hope all of these serve to establish a baseline of where we are at now. I trust our memories to fill in the gaps from here, and that the articles have inspired you to pay a little more attention to astrology, both for spiritual purposes and mundane subjects. I am biased, it is always a good idea to take a look at what is going on in the skies so you can make informed choices on how to proceed. After all, it is easier to ride a rocket ship than to constantly reinvent the wheel. The easiest way to follow along with the astrology of things is to make it part of your daily routine, in a fashion similar to checking the weather.

This chapter brings to a close the first section of the book. All of this has been background and preliminary material to set the stage for the festivals of the year. There are a few more new topics to be introduced that we will get to later. Suffice, for now, we are ready to begin. The dry material is mostly out of the way, and now we can hopefully liven things up. In the next chapters we will be taking a look at the eight festivals, highlighting and discussing key points to keep in mind that reveal the sublime rhythms and connections they all share. While the book technically wraps up after the festivals, there is an appendix, and I arranged it this way for quick reference when you need it.

CHAPTER FOUR
IMBOLC/LUGHNASADH

Looking at these festivals chronologically from the start of the calendar year, means our first one is on February 1st, and is Imbolc or Lughnasadh, depending on what you believe. Immediately, we have an important point to discuss, which is the date. Calendars and tradition will tell you this festival day is February 1st, but is it, really?

The dates for the solstices and equinoxes are basically set in stone. Not the specific days of course, rather when they occur as astronomical conditions are met. I want to draw your attention to the fluidity of the four fixed-sign festival dates. There are three different ways to calculate them which may sound intimidating, but I assure you they are not. These methods are worth looking at because they put you in a position of empowerment regarding when you honor these festivals. Just because you choose to use one method now doesn't mean you can't or won't change your mind later, or even use more than one method for more than one reason.

Imbolc/Lughnasadh are known as Fire Festivals, and long ago they were considered to be among the four most important festivals, with the equinoxes and solstices being secondary in potency. Something else to consider is the fact that the four fixed-sign fire festivals are more communal and social in nature, whereas solstices and equinoxes are more religious and spiritually focused. I get this from a cursory look at archaeology. If you look at the bulk of astrological sites they align with solstices and equinoxes rather than other events such as the first harvest. And because of this, many of the sites used for solstices and equinoxes show signs of a transient population rather than a permanent one, yet the four fixed-sign fire festivals were usually held in towns and cities that were always populated.

Now, thanks to calendars really, solstices and equinoxes are seen as equally powerful, if not more so, because they mark the beginning of the seasons. Right?

The answer to that question is a matter of opinion. Allow me to explain. There are three ways to determine the days of the four festivals that are not solstices or equinoxes. The first way is to just go by the calendar. Most calendars and websites have the dates listed. You can use those dates just fine, and really, that is the easy way.

The second method is that each of these four festivals happen at fifteen degrees of a fixed sign. As you can see, this is a little harder to understand because you have to know basic astrology to use this method.

Astrologically speaking, a season is ninety degrees long, which equates to about three months. Fifteen degrees of a fixed sign (Aquarius, Taurus, Leo, and Scorpio) is smack dab in the middle of those seasons. Each astrological sign is thirty degrees, so fifteen degrees of a fixed sign is about forty-five degrees into the season, which is a month and a half in from the beginning. So, to use this method, you have to consult an ephemeris or website that has the degrees of the sun listed on any given day. The easy rule of thumb that can save you some time is that on average, the sun moves a degree each day. This means you can already estimate when the festivals will occur. This is known as the astrological festival day, or some such similar phrase.

The third method is related to that method but is slightly different and highly pedantic. This may seem confusing because in method number two I gave the degrees for each season, however this third method takes something detailed into account. In the previous paragraph I stated that on average the sun moves a degree a day.

Sometimes the sun moves slightly more than that, and sometimes slightly less. It is not perfect, like clockwork, because we do not have a circular orbit around the sun – rather, our orbit is elliptical, which means it has a slight wobble to it. Hence, this third method says to sit down, count the number of degrees in the season, divide by two, and that is your festival day. This does usually line up with the second method, although there can be a variance of a day or two. Like method two, this method tells us the festival day will vary from year to year but will always be around the same time in the calendar. It is only recently I have learned this third method, and I point that out to show how obscure it is. I do feel it is valid and I include it here for the sake of completeness. Effectively, this third method is a tangent from the second.

Is there a correct date? No. Whichever method you choose to use is up to you, and there are pros and cons of each. You are allowed to change your mind as you grow spiritually. Or you can use more than one method at the same time.

I will give you an example from my own experience to illustrate the point. For many years when I was active in the community, I used both method number one and method number two.

The way that I did it was to engage in public events during the calendar day festivals and complete my private work on the astrological date. Use this line of thinking to work outside the box if you choose.

Before discussing the festival, there is one other point to address, and that is the imbalance regarding which ones are more powerful.

In today's world we recognize the two solstices and equinoxes as the start of each season, but to people who lived hundreds of years ago, that was not the case. To them, the four fixed-sign festivals were the more important and powerful ones. Imbolc is a perfect example of this, and since it is first on our list, we will start there.

Imbolc, no matter where you are on the planet, is the time of the first thaw from winter, or the first stirrings of spring if you live in a place that does not have a thaw, per se. Imbolc is the sign that the world didn't end with winter, rather, new life is starting to stir in the bosom of the Earth. These are signs that are observable in nature, and centuries ago when this phenomenon was noticed, the festival of Imbolc would be observed. The festival would almost always last more than a day. After all, in those times, communication and travel were not as instant or convenient as now.

So, it took a while to get the word out about the festival, and then travel time would have to be allowed for, too. Because of this, the festivals would last a week or more, and was the central activity in the area.

When you think about this you can see how these dates are, or were, the greater festivals. Survival was pre-eminent, and therefore when you saw these signs, you knew that the times they were a-changin'. That would put the following solstice or equinox as the height of the season, not the beginning of it. In modern times this is flipped, I am sure we have all experienced a season occurring before the calendar says it is supposed to start, so there is some validity here.

An experiment you can do is to look at the physical world signs in your neighborhood and see how they line up with the festival itself. If you took a literal approach, how would that differ to tradition? For example, there are parts of the world that won't see their first bloom or sprout for quite a while after other places, so how would this affect the wheel of the year? Unless you're living at an extreme latitude, things should line up close to tradition. For example, if tradition says February 1st, then that means you could see the first stirrings of spring anywhere from late January to the second week in February.

Of course, there is variance, and an uncomfortable truth that should be kept in mind, which is climate change. Climate change can affect these first stirrings and buddings. I have not found this to be a rule of thumb, rather a theory that I have explored and found correct more often than not. In recent years I have paid attention to this more out of professional curiosity rather than anything else. I've learned a lot about rhythms and how they apply to the wheel of the year, but I have not really put this into practice as you might expect. That is because I have drawn the laziness line in the sand there. I've researched it and seen its validity but have not put it into practice for a year. If you're curious, check it out and see how your wheel of the year will vary from what is printed. Experimentation is the way forward, after all.

There is one more point I would like to clarify before we continue. In the introduction I said that another term for this wheel is The Witches' Wheel, or The Witches' Wheel of the Year. Today you do find these terms in common usage, and what I would like to point out is that these festivals are not restricted to witches. Most, if not all, witches work with these festivals, however many other traditions honor them as well. This includes druids, ceremonial magicians, and many others who do not even fall under the Neopagan umbrella.

I have known many people over the years who are simply Earth-based in their spirituality and do not necessarily align with the principles and practices of Neopagans; they recognize the point and function of these times and have decided to incorporate them into their spiritual practices.

A newer spiritual tradition, Christo-Paganism, even goes so far as to align Christianity with these festivals. You will see below how they are historically intertwined, and in modern practice this intertwining goes further.

Generally, today, the traditional and Neopagan practices of the festivals largely stay the same, only Jesus, Mary, and other characters from the Abrahamic mythos are substituted in place of more Pagan and traditional deities such as Brigid, Cernunnos, etc. I feel all of this is necessary to point out and explain because these practices and festivals are not closed to outside practitioners. Some spiritual systems are, but these are not, for various reasons, the biggest of which is that all eight festivals come from various places and have been interwoven over centuries, creating a singular system for all of us to use.

Imbolc

This is the festival that denotes winter is coming to an end, and the first stirrings of spring are occurring. In this way it is the true beginning of spring. The calendar day for Imbolc in the northern hemisphere is February 1st, and in the southern hemisphere it is August 1st. There are different names for this festival that should be noted. Sometimes you will see it spelled as Imbolg because of translation differences, and an alternative name for it is Candlemas. Technically, Candlemas falls on February 2nd, not the 1st, but then again, I have seen Imbolc listed as February 2nd, too, so they are happening at the same time, metaphysically speaking.

Candlemas is a Christian holy day with several different names, too. It predominantly has to do with presenting Jesus to the temple when he was young. It gets its name from the practice that many Christians have – taking their candles, left over from the previous holy days, to the church to get blessed for the upcoming year. Candles play an important role in the Pagan festival, too. The Celtic goddess Brigid is seen as the goddess associated with this time because her feast day is February 2nd, and she is a fire goddess, hence the candles connection. This also means the Christian St Brigid's feast day is held at this time.

The making of a Brigid's cross is a common practice, as is the burning of candles, and indulging in milk or using it as an offering. A Brigid's cross is an equal armed cross usually woven together from reeds or other plants like that. However, it can technically be made of anything. Mine is made from wood, for example. The Brigid's cross is a protective symbol and is usually hung over a door.

The milk correspondence comes from a noticed natural phenomenon around this time – this was the time of year that animals started lactating, which meant they were basically ready to go for the upcoming year. This reinforces how natural occurrences were noticed and celebrated, and how tradition was built. I always laugh when I think about this. I can imagine one farmer walking his fence line standing there, talking to his neighbor who is doing the same. The first farmer asks the second, "Cow lactating?" to which the second responds, "Yep," and the first replies, "Guess it's time for Imbolc," and they both nod and go about their ways. What a romanticized picture of the past.

Imbolc is the first light of spring that brings with it the promise of renewal. The previous season of winter brought death and incubation. Before education was widespread and when science, as we know it, didn't exist, it was an actual question every year that people had: Was winter the end? As in, the end of everything? Consequently, the following spring arrived to let people know that everything would open back up. Of course, eventually people saw that nature lived in patterns and cycles, and with the development of the natural sciences, people learned to move away from unsubstantiated fears like that. People still fear the unknown without reason today, but it is less common than it was centuries ago. Various cultures wove stories about why this occurred, and the descent of the goddess into the underworld immediately comes to mind. During the cold months, a common story was that the goddess who brought life and warmth to the planet was in the underworld, and her influence was lacking. With Imbolg we see the first signs that she will be returning soon, to make things right.

It is important to look at these four fire festivals, in particular Imbolc, through the lens of your local environment. To follow a point from earlier, let's discuss lactating animals as an example. What if you live in an area where this doesn't happen, or at least isn't common? Ok, then look at other behaviors that occur around this time and make them part of your festival experience.

Every climate on Earth (yes, even deserts) have changes that happen when the seasons change. They might be barely noticeable, but they are still there, so it might take you some time to learn and experience these things – they are worth it for aligning with the seasons in your area. If you do this for an extended period of time, what kind of cycles do you notice? What kind of variance is there if you watch this for five years in a row? Ten? If you take this approach you can get a better understanding of the cycle of the year, but you don't have context to truly process your observances and results. If you use this practice for a few years, you create a larger sample size to draw inferences and conclusions from, which means your thoughts will be more grounded in context.

Imbolc doesn't mean that it is the time to plant seeds, rather that you are at the point where it is only a matter of time before the ground will be ready for planting. For now, it is enough to know that spring is unfolding. Another festival on the horizon will be the time to plant seeds, and it is not that far away. This is a good time to take an inventory of your stores.

Did you have enough to get through the winter? Where were you lacking, and how do you address that going forward?

What is ready to go for the upcoming year?

What can you do to prepare for the upcoming new astrological year?

What is out of your control?

These and related questions are the ones to ask now. The only real challenge to this is to avoid getting caught up in minutia.

Lammas / Lughnasadh

Besides being known as Lammas, this festival is also known as Lughnasadh or Loaf Mass. Like Candlemas, Loaf Mass is a Christian holy day, and in Christian traditions, a loaf of bread is taken to church to be blessed during a mass to celebrate the first harvest. This also extends to Christian priests blessing local bakeries for continued success, and a donation, I'm sure!

The title Lammas comes from Old English and is basically the combination of Loaf Mass. Loaf Mass shortened to Lammas in that dialect. This is simply worth noting as a point of historical accuracy. From time to time the historicity of the festivals and their names comes up, so I offer this here as clarification.

While Wicca is a new invention that incorporates old festivals, many of the facts we will discuss in this section are historical and not new inventions.

The codification of these seasonal celebrations into one wheel of the year is a new structure but these celebrations existed on their own for centuries.

Aligning the eight festival days occurred in the early part of the twentieth century at the hands of Gerald Gardner and Ross Nichols, and the name, Wheel of the Year, came from the 1960s and the occult revival that was occurring.

Lughnasadh comes from the Gaelic tradition and celebrates the beginning of harvest season. Additionally, this is a very interesting festival because it has the name of a deity in its title, which is the Irish god Lugh. Lugh is the god of light, the sun, and craftsmen. He is also known as a warrior, king, and savior. He corresponds to truth and the law. It is unclear which name came first but it is widely and commonly suspected that Lughnasadh came first, since it has Pagan roots. This was a common practice of Christianity – to choose holy days at or around the same time as indigenous Pagan festivals in order to easily convert the population.

Many religions older than Christianity engaged in this practice too, although they are not as recent in our collective memory, and generally, the only thing that was changed were the names of the deities.

A great example of this is Sumeria and Mesopotamia. Not only did they leave the places and dates the same, the only thing they changed were the names of the deities. The Romans and the Greeks are another good example of this; the religious practices of both predate Christianity, and were also largely regional, whereas Christianity was global, making the scope that much larger and more damaging.

The idea is the same in both, to honor the beginning of harvest. However, Lughnasadh was a step grander, including more activities than gluten-based ones. Lughnasadh included trading, ceremonies, matchmaking, and athletic games of prowess.

The way I like to think of it is to consider that this festival was probably the first Olympic Games, before even the Greeks, who made them famous. Offerings of food were common, as was animal sacrifice.

It is widely suspected that in the oldest of times, this included human sacrifice, but from what I can tell, that is speculation that comes from the connection between the head cult and Lughnasadh. I won't get into the head cult here, but for those of you who have a knack for obscurities, I encourage you to check it out.

This festival was the traditional time for people to enter into year-and-a-day agreements with each other. While this usually has to do with romantic relationships, it can also be aimed at projects or relationships with deities. For example, my astrology workbook is set up as a year-and-a-day format, but it begins on the equinox rather than on this date.

People often enter into commitments with deities that last a year and a day, and these can be anything from pledging to work with a deity for a year and a day, all the way to entering into a spirit marriage for a year and a day as a kind of test run to see what a longer-term relationship might look like.

The calendar date for this is August 1st, and astrologically it happens halfway between summer solstice and autumn equinox in the northern hemisphere, which is usually fifteen degrees of the fixed fire-sign, Leo. Some modern practices celebrate the festival the Sunday beforehand, and this underscores the point that these ancient festivals lasted a number of days instead of one. I have even seen some practitioners start their observances on July 31st instead of August 1st.

In many ancient cultures the new year began with the sun moving into Leo, which happens a few days before Lughnasadh.

You find this point of paramount importance when studying Chaldea, the Chaldean Oracles, and many other sublime systems in the Western Esoteric Tradition. A version of this was true in ancient Egypt, where the year began with the rising of the star Sirius, which usually occurred a few days before the traditional calendar date of Lughnasadh.

Ancient Egyptians rectified this by adding five epagomenal days to the calendar and attributed them to the birth of some of their gods.

The Egyptians did this because of the rising of the fixed star Sirius, and how it coincided with the flooding of the Nile – other cultures did it for other reasons. When you see a cycle in ceremonial magick that begins with the astrological sign Leo, or on August 1st as we know it today, then you now know there is some of this influence present.

As a matter of fact, you could even go so far as to say that this approach dates back to around 10,500 BCE, when the sphinx gazed at its invisible counterpart Leo rising in the eastern sky, but that is a deeper conversation for another time.

You can see that these two festivals have to do with gratitude in one form or another.

Imbolc because you are grateful that you made it through the winter, and Lughnasadh because you are starting to see the fruits of your harvest from the work you've done throughout the year. The nice thing about Lughnasadh is that if you take a tally of your stores at this harvest, you still have time to make adjustments before the upcoming winter, so in this way it is not only gratitude for what has been done, it is also a warning of what is to come if you are not prepared enough.

Both of these also have to do with light, like the other two fixed-sign festivals, and I point this out because you can give them quite liberal interpretations and correspondences, especially when it comes to deities. The first one that comes to mind is Lucifer, although any solar deities can be worked with during these festivals. The other four festivals have to do with either balance or extremes, hence deities who are aligned with those concepts are more appropriate. Specifically, the equinoxes are well-suited for balance deities, winter solstice is appropriate for dark deities, and summer solstice for light ones in general, but not necessarily light deities that have to do with the sun or light itself. An example of a light deity that does not correspond to light or the sun would be Quan Yin.

The other two fire festivals, which we will discuss more in-depth later in this book, are also connected with fire and light, although not necessarily in the same way as these two. Both Beltane and Samhain are considered fire festivals, but neither one predominantly focuses on gratitude in the way that these two do. You could make the case that Samhain focuses on gratitude in the sense that honoring the ancestors is part of it, but that is really the only part that aligns with gratitude, and even then, the ancestors are honored, not ingratiated, although many interchange the two. Beltane does not focus on gratitude though.

As an aside, while gratitude can be added to these festivals, it is not an intrinsic part of them, historically speaking. Light is another difference between the Imbolc/Lughnasadh axis of festivals and the Beltane/Samhain axis.

The concept of light is found in Imbolc, Lughnasadh, and Beltane, but not in Samhain, traditionally speaking.

An important point to note is that just because a fire festival incorporates fire it does not necessarily mean it incorporates light. Magically speaking, light and fire are separate concepts, even though we know how the two are connected.

We're through the first axis of festivals we are discussing, and I hope you see how this axis is connected, and how it differs from the other one we'll discuss soon. It is far too easy to lump all fire festivals into the same category, but there are nuanced differences to take into account. When planning for each festival, I have found that it is the details that matter, many times more than the generalities. Details personalize the festival and ritual experiences, providing a three-dimensional manifestation of one's path, and bringing one's goals into dynamic results.

CHAPTER FIVE
OSTARA/MABON

Now we move onto the equinox axis of Ostara and Mabon, the spring and autumn equinoxes respectively. Although a lot of this has been discussed previously, now we will turn our attention to more subtleties. The first is that Ostara is also known as the vernal equinox, and International Astrology Day.

When I am doing magical projects, or self-improvement projects, I rarely start on January first. After all, I live in the northern hemisphere, and that date is winter, so it makes no sense to begin something new in the middle of winter. We are already in the Kali Yuga, so why make it harder on myself? I usually wait until spring equinox because that is when the energetic year truly begins.

Yes, this means that the current calendar we use, the Gregorian calendar, doesn't make sense. It follows traditions found throughout the western world, and that's about it. If a calendar was going to be truly done right, it would be done in line with the astrological year, meaning it would start on spring equinox.

You can see the problem; if you did this, the calendar would favor the northern hemisphere. Then again, so many things do already.

I point this out because when we are executing projects and rituals, we are connecting the microcosm with the macrocosm, the self with the greater, and what better time to do that than the spring equinox? Remember, the spring equinox in the southern hemisphere is in September, not March, so this means the September equinox is known as the vernal equinox in the south, and that also applies for International Astrology Day if you live below the equator. When looking at things personally and magically, it is wise to line up with what is happening astrologically and not the calendar. You can use the calendar if you want, but that is putting the ego before the energetic.

Ostara

Ostara is the name of a western Germanic spring goddess, and parallels to her can be found all over the globe. Another goddess comes to mind here, which is the goddess Eostre, who is the Anglo-Saxon parallel. When looking at working with the wheel of the year it is wise to do your research to see what goddess is applicable to you and your location.

These two are also the roots of the modern-day word Easter, found in the Christian faith. This is considered the beginning of spring, and thus the theme of the festival is obvious. This is a time of new beginnings.

It is considered the return of the goddess from the underworld, where she has remained for several months. Hence, this is also a time of renewal as much as it is a time of new beginnings.

Environmentally, seeds are beginning to bloom, trees are leaving, and there are fewer cold temperatures as the ground wakes up to warmth and new life. Rejuvenation and resurrection are two other themes closely related which can apply here.

So, you can see why the Christian idea of the resurrection of Jesus the Christ is celebrated during this time.

That is their way of aligning with older traditions, which is a good lesson in metaphysics. You can change up names and images of themes found during these festivals to whatever your spiritual paradigm is, and as long as the themes and images align with the energy of the festival, you're good to go.

Abundance is another trait of this festival, and it is time to extrapolate on this a bit. Abundance and prosperity are two radically different concepts, even though they are often linked together. The easy way to understand the difference is to know basic financial concepts and terms. Prosperity is when you have a high profit margin, whereas abundance is when you have what you need as well as some surplus. Ostara is a festival day of abundance, and this makes sense, logically. Coming out of winter, the first thing one does is assess where they are financially, personally, and spiritually.

How did you navigate the winter? Where is your surplus? Where is your lack? And, once the assessment is done, where do you go from here?

Stagnation equals death, so it doesn't make any sense to maintain the status quo unless that is the best you can manage.

This means that during Ostara, it is a good time to bring something new into being, which reveals that this is a festival of birth and fertility. It is not as focused on sex as other festivals, rather on being fertile enough to start new projects.

Because of this, Ostara is also known as a festival of creativity, which is reflected in the variety of bright colors associated with it.

Emotionally, this is a festival of joy and happiness – we survived the winter! The time of renewal is at hand, reminding us that everything is cyclical. As a dear friend of mine once told me, "that which dies can be resurrected, but that which is changed, is changed forever."

Everything has a cycle, an important point to note, because so many people do not recognize this fact. As science teaches us, energy is neither created nor destroyed, it simply changes form. Hence, this proves reincarnation to be true, scientifically speaking.

All of the energy contained in your body and consciousness will one day change away from the form and mind that you know, and when that day comes, it will morph into something else.

What that is, no one knows, and ultimately a lot of the answer is subjective and open to interpretation. Of course, this is all my opinion, I hope the logic demonstrates the validity of reincarnation.

When it comes to practices for Ostara, there is a wide variety of what you can choose. As long as your practices have to do with birth, rebirth, creativity, and new beginnings, you are on the right track. A traditional practice that was adapted to mainstream culture is that of colored eggs.

This isn't the only practice of course, although it is one of the more popular ones that has endured. Another practice present at Ostara is planting seeds, regardless of whether they sprout into flowers. Bonfires are also common, as are flowers in general. I separate them here from the seeds because you can use flowers that are already in existence, rather than waiting for new ones to grow. Connecting with nature is also good to do at this time, whether it is meditating in nature or simply spending time outside.

Mabon

Mabon is the common name given to the autumn equinox. Of course, the month of this festival varies depending on which hemisphere you inhabit. Taking its name from a character in Welsh mythology, Mabon represents the completion of harvest season.

The toil of the year is not only done for the most part, it has also been tallied, and preparations are being made for the upcoming winter season.

What I find interesting about this festival is that its existence implies the belief in reincarnation, because it is at this point in the year that the recognition of cycles is occurring. What was alive is decaying and dying, only to be born again in a little while.

I find it hard to understand a Pagan who practices the wheel of the year who does not believe in reincarnation, because the entire year is based around cycles and rebirth, but that is just me.

Inventory is a word that corresponds to this festival too, and I find it highly disturbing that the application of taking an inventory is absent in occultism and modern spirituality today. Taking an inventory of something means seeing what you've got. How good was your return on your investment? If you planted six seeds, did you end up with six plants, more than that, or fewer?

All of these things matter because without taking an inventory we have no way to chart our progress and successes.

Maybe the time we planted them was wrong, or right, if the results are more than we expected. Or maybe where we planted the seeds was the wrong place. Or perhaps we didn't nurture them enough. Without answering these and related questions, we have no idea how good or bad we are, both in the physical world and in the spiritual.

Mabon draws our attention to this. The harvest is done. There will be no more fruits of our labor. What do we have? How did we do?

This is the festival to assess. In this way you could call it a time of judgment, the time of great balancing which is definitely in line with the equinox. When assessing, it is key to practice self-compassion, so we do not degrade our ego. Just because something didn't work out now doesn't mean it won't work out in the future. And just because we yielded something more than we planted, doesn't mean it will always be that way. By assessing what we've created, we can see where and how we can improve.

Symbolically, this is the beginning of the descent of the goddess into the underworld – and remember that she returns at Ostara. This six-month period is when temperatures are the coldest and the world seems to be dying.

We now know that it will be reborn but in ancient times that would have been in question. For those of you who work with dark goddesses, or goddesses who travel to the underworld, this is your time. Solar goddesses, dawn goddesses, and the like, all correspond to the previous time period of Ostara until Mabon.

The descent of Inanna comes to mind here, although there are other myths from other cultures that are similar that can equally apply. This reinforces the constant theme of reading the myths of your spiritual tradition.

Astrologically, this is a good festival to put on your radar because things are changing. Not only is the planet dying, there are significant events that cyclically happen. The first is that shortly after this festival, most of the significant planets in the solar system move direct, if they are not already. It is also around this time that the second pair of eclipses happen.

To further illustrate this point, below is an article I wrote which I hope illustrates why it is wise to start paying closer attention to the stars as Mabon approaches.

All Systems Go!

Excerpt from an article originally published in the *Dolmen Grove Chronicles* in October, 2018

The middle of October brings us to a powerful moment in this astrological year. After months of many retrogrades occurring continually, we have a 'full steam ahead' energy in the air. Finally! A minimum of six planets at a time have been retrograde for quite a while now, by mid-October, that number is reduced to three: Uranus, Chiron, and Neptune. Chiron and Neptune go direct in December, so long story short, it's time to move forward. The period of inner reflection comes to a close, and it is time to shift our attention to what we choose to manifest in our physical lives.

In a lot of ways, this may be counter-intuitive to how we practice in the west. In the northern hemisphere, it is autumn. The planet is performing its annual decaying and cleansing period before the upcoming winter, where the final stages of annual death will occur, only to rejuvenate again in the spring with new life and opportunities. Therefore, when I mention that it is all systems go, it may be seen as being in direct opposition to the natural cycles of life, but is it, really?

In the southern hemisphere, this is the spring season, which corresponds to new beginnings and, you guessed it, moving ahead full steam. In this light, we can see that the astrological energy in the air favors those who live in the southern hemisphere, as cosmic energy can produce larger than expected results. So, for those of you reading this who live in the southern hemisphere, enjoy this especially strong spring! For those of us in the north, it is time to cut through this apparent paradox of energies.

As we move into the decaying and dying part of the year in the northern hemisphere, the energy becomes more conducive to letting go and tallying what we have produced this year to prepare for the upcoming winter. When extended, this also means preparing for the upcoming spring, when the cycle begins anew, and we can integrate what we have learned from this year.

When we put two and two together, we see that now it is time to get proactive and prepare for next year. Now is the time to assess what has occurred this year and apply what we have learned. If we ponder this, we also see that we can infer that all of this layered energy means that things will come up in the next two months that will prevent us from completing our assessment when we normally would.

So, in essence, we prepare now, and then over the next few months, that assessment and those plans get put on hold for various reasons subjective to our personal paradigms. So, as we assess this year, we also see what needs to be changed to have a more successful year in 2022.

We will now turn our attention to the specifics. After all, everything I just shared above are broad strokes at the big picture, so it stands to reason we should look at the particulars.

First, Mercury directs on October 18th, which means it is a good time to plan for your future success, now that so much has been dealt with and assessed. Secondly, the sun moves into Scorpio on October 23rd, so the energy in the air lends itself towards intensity, focus, and drive. Saturn went direct on October 11th, so it is wise to lay the foundation for the next calendar year in the northern hemisphere and the astrological new year in the south. Pluto also went direct on October 6th, so it is now time to take your inner transformation and apply it to your relationship with the outside world. Finally, on October 31st, Hallow's Eve, Mars enters its sign of Scorpio.

While this is good for increased energy levels, it may be too much of a good thing, and tempers and accidents may become more common.

This increased activity in Scorpio comes into conflict with Saturn and Jupiter in Aquarius. Saturn and Jupiter are known as the social planets, and Aquarius is known as the sign of groups and, in many ways, the greater society at large. Thus, we see that it would be wise to make adjustments with who we are and where we are going, and how that may conflict with the will of social consciousness. Both Scorpio and Aquarius are fixed signs, meaning that stubbornness may produce a lot of this friction, so being open-minded and flexible are two ways you can come into alignment with the greater whole. Scorpio can be seen as a sign of self-focus, much like Leo, but Aquarius can focus on what the group wants rather than the individual. On the surface, this may seem like the two foci conflict, however that idea is an illusion.

Let us look at a couple of examples to illustrate the point. The first one that comes to mind is the idea of social justice. All of this is hypothetical, so you may have to ponder this to extract the principle. Group consciousness may be implying that now is the time to change the toxic parts of social justice, while you may feel that change is not necessary.
Well, at least not the kind of change that the group wants. Superficially, this may look as though the will of the individual and the will of the group conflict but actually, they both want

the same thing: fair justice across the board. So, the individual may be tempted to fight the will of the whole, however the smarter course of action would be to accept that change is the only constant, and that change can be guided and sometimes altered or diverted into more personal areas. Learning how to be diplomatic and focused on compromise would be the way to achieve success in this example.

Another example that illustrates this point is to ponder the connection between the past and the present. Aquarius is a future-oriented sign, whereas Scorpio generally corresponds to the tried-and-true methods rooted in the past.

Many years ago, I would keep a paper and pencil ledger of the financial side of my business (Scorpio). Over time and with experience I upgraded to using a computer (Aquarius). In the air is the energy of transforming the old into the new, the traditional into the visionary. It is not so much a case of which is wrong or right, rather it is a case of progress versus stagnation, and the question one has to ask oneself is, which part of history will I be on?

Trying to stagnate things to keep outdated methods alive, or be part of the group of people bringing the future into manifested reality?

As Dion Fortune said, to paraphrase, the examples may become outdated but the principles are timeless.

We also find that attention shifts away from dealing with personal relationships, which has been the case for a lot of August, all of September, and early October. We can see the magical shift from the microcosm to the macrocosm and the individual's relationship with it. In that regard, we see that it all comes back to the Hermetic axiom, like so many other magical concepts, "As above, so below, as within, so without."

As we move further into the next season, it is wise to contemplate this as it can serve as a beacon to show us how we should grow through evolution, whether the people in the situations stay the same or change. After all, one of the best ways to see change unfold is to be present during the transitional process. Turning a blind eye is akin to burying one's head in the sand, and only serves to damage the individual.

*

Let's follow that article up with another one taken from the same source. The way it ties into our discussion is that it discusses the time period between the equinoxes, Mabon and

Ostara, and also points to the fact that so much of our reality is colored by our imagination. I can tell you that this is the descent of the goddess into the underworld, but what does that mean to you? Do you have a goddess in your pantheon that illustrates this idea? Or do you look at this more existentially, seeing this as a time to go within, descending into the arena of the mind and the subconscious? Or do you practice both?

Regardless, the language and imagery you use to describe this time determines your reality, and therefore can have a profound impact on activating your imagination, which is the alchemist's playground.

Life is Poetry in Motion

Excerpt from an article originally published in the *Dolmen Grove Chronicles* on Samhain, 2018.

This may seem like an odd title for an article about astrology, however, I assure you all things will be made clear.
The title for this article works on the very simple premise that all things are fluid, yet poetic at the same time.

Therefore, what we are effectively doing is painting our mark on the greater tapestry of this paradigm. As the American author, Henry David Thoreau, pointed out, the world is but a tapestry for our imagination. All things are fluid, there is a rhythm and a reason for everything, and nothing is static. If yesterday's villains are today's heroes, then today's pains are tomorrow's pleasures.

This fits into the current astrological position due to the fact that we are coming out of a month of eight retrogrades in the sky, resulting in a lot of personal changes.

When planets are retrograde, it means there is an internal focus on our personal qualities. Therefore, most will have been inwardly focused and making changes accordingly. Or, they have been living in denial, which is their right. In either case, a lot of people have been focused on internal growth.

However, the reaper requires payment, hence the need for us to make the necessary changes. This has led to many people coming out of August changed, scarred, or in a state of bliss; the latter being brought about by ignorance.
I don't know of one person that came out of August unchanged. The reason for this is important – it is because we are about to enter the second half of the zodiacal year.

These first six signs have been intense, to say the least, so what will the next six bring? More of the same? Or something more balancing?

The next six months are going to balance things out from these last six months, so for those of you that have had an interesting time of it, I can tell you things will calm down a bit.

Does this mean that things are going to become placid and smooth? Of course not. There is no 'mutually exclusive' when it comes to astrology. We still have a Mercury retrograde and various other retrogrades, stationings, full moon and new moon cycles, so there is still a lot that can occur.

However, you can watch for things to quieten down substantially and the focus to be shifted. For the next few months, you can expect the emphasis to be on opportunities where you can demonstrate what you have learned.

We just experienced an equinox, a time of balance which occurs no matter where you are physically located on the planet. In the northern hemisphere it is the autumn equinox, and in the southern it is the spring or vernal equinox. Regardless of where you are, this is a profound period and opportunity to bring about balance within the self.

The way this relates to the title of the article is that we will now experience the second half of the poetic verse.

Were the first six months of your astrological year turbulent? If so, this will balance them out. However, if the first six months of your astrological year have been quiet, this will balance them out. This is the lesson for the entire astrological year, it's just that the first six months were the prepay for what is coming.

I don't want to sugarcoat things and leave you thinking that it will be rainbows and light on the horizon because it will not, instead I want to give a sense of reality. While now is the time when things will be balanced out, despite our perceptions and beliefs, likewise the next six months will be balanced regardless of how we think they should be balanced. That, my friends, is the bitter pill to swallow. The trick, as Buddha told us, is to see our thoughts as a river, yet remain detached from what we see.

Going into the next six months of the astrological year, we now know what to expect, and it would be in poor taste and ignorance to get upset at situations that we perceive to work against us, because in fact these situations are occurring to balance things out in some way, shape, or form.

Hence, if we get upset at something, the first thing we should do is look into the mirror and practice the Hermetic axiom, As Within, So Without.

For example, if we think we were wronged in a situation yet the next few weeks bring us headaches, then we should put our ego aside and focus on the facts at hand. If karma is saying we screwed up, regardless of what we think, then we screwed up, and we should internally work on understanding this and working with it.

Our perception of the situations in our lives should come secondary to what is happening around us. After all, this is the scientific method of thinking.

We should perceive and interpret what we see in order to extrapolate the wisdom. In this way, life is poetry because of the serendipity involved.

However, it is a great life lesson in the way the world works, and the next few months will provide a window of opportunity for reflection, and this reflection can produce the information for what to expect during the next half of the zodiacal year.

In the course of this reflection, one should be honest in their assessment. Being egocentric would be detrimental to the cause.

If you've been out of balance, now is the time to right the scales. If things have been out of balance in your life, now is the time things will correct themselves. A lot of this will happen naturally, but it is wise to assist, where possible, by letting go of the things that no longer serve you in some way. The discernment test is to know what to release and what to keep, although I'm sure you have figured that out by now. After all, discretion is the better part of valor.

The really cool secret is that the way we release and the way we keep are both strokes of the same brush of our Will on the tapestry of the world. Some people let go of things compassionately, others are brasher in their approach. In truth it doesn't matter how you do it, simply know that however you choose to do this, it is your brush stroke on the tapestry of the psyche of the human mind, so it would be wise to plan accordingly. An unspoken concept in astrology is that things which are happening now will be an inverted reflection of what will be occurring six months from now, because this six-month cycle happens to everyone all the time, which means that all of us are stronger than we may realize.

If we pay attention to these intermediate cycles, we find that a lot of power is within our control if we seize the day, or night as the case may be. In this way we can look backwards to six months ago to see how things will be balanced and harmonized again. We can also understand that our own behavior will, to some extent, dictate what is coming up six months from now. So, look at how you were living six months ago, and then look back five years ago. Those two things will tell you what to expect for the next six months.

Choose how you want to paint the next six months, while considering what five years into the future might hold if you continue on your regular journey.

*

I hope these articles illustrate what to expect during this axis and how much of a role our imagination plays in the spiritual arts. Developing your imagination is something that can be a very powerful tool during your spiritual journey.

As I like to think of it, if the weather is bad out, then why challenge it? That doesn't make any sense. It is better to do inner work, both within yourself and within your home, during the part of the year that runs from Mabon to Ostara.

How this is done takes many forms, so there is no one-size-fits-all approach. I tell you this so that if you encounter those who say there is only one way to proceed, then be warned they are misleading you. The only one-size-fits-all approach is that this is the time of decay, dying, and eventually rebirth. Past that, it's up to you.

At this point it is wise to remind you of your personal mythology. What is your myth? Who are your heroes? What stories do you have to tell, and what wisdom have you learned from living through them? This axis is an excellent time to address these and related questions. If you need help structuring this, then dive into the structure of the wheel. There are major characters and concepts that run through all eight festivals.

For example, the goddess ruling the world and then descending into the underworld, only to be born again. If you are a woman, has this happened to you? If you are a man, have you found damnation and salvation through the role of a woman in your life?

These festivals are more than just celebrations to honor the seasons. They are also prime times for passion plays, and what better material to draw on than your own life?

I have found value in putting life experiences up against Joseph Campbell's journey of a hero motif, or the formula of the living, dying, resurrected god. There is a lot of material on this approach, and some good places to start are the writings of Joseph Campbell, Dr Carl Jung, and classical mythology tales, such as the Greek myths, that have morals and messages in them. Once you've got a handle on processing your life through this kind of thinking, there is only one thing left to do, which is create a ritual or rituals that act as psychological tools for your greatest growth and good.

CHAPTER SIX
BELTANE/SAMHAIN

Now we move onto one of the more popular axes, which is the one between Beltane and Samhain. Both are fire festivals, and some could argue that Samhain has grown beyond its Pagan roots and evolved into a mainstream tradition with the advent of Halloween in civilized countries. To understand this axis takes a little bit of explaining, because we are not just talking about a single event. Rather we are talking about a festival that begins at nightfall of the previous day and lasts through the following day. This may seem contradictory to what I said earlier about these festivals lasting for longer than a day at a time, so bear with me as I explain how it is in modern times, but not necessarily as it was in older times, as established earlier. We'll start with Beltane.

Beltane

If not for a couple of outstanding events, Beltane may have fallen to the popularity of Lughnasadh or Imbolc. One of the events is a long-held tradition of the Maypole, which has occurred outside of specifically Pagan realms for a long, long time.

Many places have kept the tradition of the Maypole long after the festival it was associated with was lost. The other event is much more commercial, which is the movie *The Wicker Man*. This classic was released at a time when all things related to occultism were at the forefront of the cultural evolution happening in the western world. Regardless of authenticity, the movie was set during Beltane, drawing attention to this festival. Since then, more movies have come out that have to do with sabbats, and it is because of these that many people have discovered these celebrations. This also makes things tricky, because people discover these festivals expecting them to be like they have seen in the cinema. Of course, the festivals are nothing like that, and this can lead to disappointment or interest, depending on opinion.

Beltane is a fertility festival, albeit a different kind of fertility to Ostara. The fertility of Beltane is that of pollination rather than planting. In other words, Beltane corresponds to sex, whereas Ostara is foreplay. During Ostara we plant seeds, at Beltane we fertilize them to enhance their growth cycle. This can be extrapolated out to mean that Beltane also corresponds to newness and freshness.

The seeds have been planted and now it is time to nurture them. To help you stay on track, Beltane also corresponds to seed planting.

This is more of an afterthought of a correspondence, because initial planting is done at Ostara, and the planting that is done at Beltane is that which needs warmer climes to grow. Not all seeds gestate the same. Some need warmer ground to be planted in, while others are fine to lie dormant in colder soil until the planet warms up.

Beltane is also known as May Eve, or Roodmas. Roodmas is a Christian holy day that commemorates the cross. Unlike Beltane, Roodmas has two traditional dates: May 1st and September 14th. We see a clue to the complexity with its alternate title of May Eve, because really, the festival starts the night before the 1st.

The night before is known as Walpurgisnacht, the night before the feast day of St. Walburga. Among her other traits, Walburga was known to be effective against witchcraft, and in central and northern Germany it was believed that at this time, witches flew to the grand Sabbat on Mt. Brocken, to perform works of evil.

In Bavaria this night was known as Hexennacht, or Night of the Witches, and was very similar to Halloween as it is celebrated today.

Anton Lavey, founder of the Church of Satan, found this night so influential that he started his organization on it in 1966. I mention all of this because in some ways it is the grandest sabbat of them all, yet not part of the modern wheel of the year. Technically.

Personally, I consider it the hidden, ninth sabbat, in much the same vein as the sun behind the sun, or, in some traditions, a hidden chakra. This is because I extensively work with ancient Egypt, and one of the gods there is Amun, the hidden god, which serves as a reminder that there is always something hidden.

Interestingly enough, this is a good spot for a segue into a lesser discussed topic of the wheel of the year – it's Christian alignment. We all know that Pagan practices were around for centuries before Christianity rose, and we know that whenever Christianity moved to a new area, they put their holy days on the same dates, or close to, the existing ones of the conquered people.

While they weren't the only religion to do this, they do garner particular note because they are the most recent one to do it, and we have not undone their cultural violation. At least not yet.

The point is, that for most of these festivals, the festivities began the night before the celebrated day. Keep in mind that we are largely using broad strokes to discuss this because originally these festivals lasted several days at a time and were very fluid events. If you look at the four fire festivals, you'll see that there is a celebration the evening before.

Each of these four festivals actually start after dark the night before. Beltane begins with the lighting of the Bael fire the night before, and Hallows (commonly known as Samhain), begins the night before at Hallow's eve. The reason I point this out and find it interesting is because in the Jewish faith, many holy days begin at sunset, so I find it curious that the two intersect like this. And after all, where there's smoke there's fire, but that is a conversation for another time. Suffice for now, it is enough to know that this parallel exists, making the wheel of the year more fascinating to study.

When it comes to practices associated with this festival, there are a few noteworthy ones that define Beltane.

The first is the Maypole. This is a tall wooden pole with colored strips of fabric or streamers coming off of it. At the end of each streamer is a person holding it.

The pole itself represents the phallus and the colored strips are the colors of fertility, spring and joy. While chanting, each of the participants weave the streamers together in an intricate dance, and when all is said and done, the streamers are tightly wound to the pole. This in turn is stripped from the pole and kept until the next Beltane when it is ceremonially burned in gratitude.

The second is that of bonfires. Bonfires were used in a lot of ancient festivals, and the cynic in me says it was as much for practical purposes as spiritual ones. Usually the bonfires were started the night before the festival proper, and not only were they a source of heat and light, they also served as cooking fires and for long distance communication as much as a spiritual focus. Beltane, in particular, is known for its bonfires the night before, on Walpurgisnacht, AKA Hexennacht.

The third practice commonly associated with Beltane takes a little more explanation, and this is the practice of the burning of the wicker man. According to early Roman writings, this was a large wicker structure that druids used to burn either an animal or human sacrifice. Some argue this did not occur, while others say the story is exaggerated, however in every story there is a kernel of truth. This practice was made popular by the movie *The Wicker Man*.

I simply share this practice because it has continued over the centuries, ranging from 18th century France to the present day. My guess, which is purely educated speculation, is that a semblance of this practice was common. It might or might not have included human sacrifice, might or might not have happened at Beltane, and might or might not have been a regular occurrence associated with Beltane.

To wit, this could have been a practice that varied from festival to festival, a sort of floating Pagan practice used when appropriate rather than tied to just one festival date. Regardless, in the present day and age, burning effigies regularly occurs, and more often than not, happens at Beltane.

Yes, I said human sacrifice. An uncomfortable fact is that human sacrifice did occur before the rise of Christianity and was common enough that a story was woven into the Bible to forbid the practice – Abraham sacrificing Isaac, and God saying that is wrong.

There can be no denial of ancient Pagan practices. Like Egyptian practices, human sacrifices were practiced by Pagan peoples, and while times have changed, we should not deny where we've come from.

In the following article, written for release in the middle of May, I address some of the common themes that come up around Beltane. Like all things astrological, there is a lot of variance that can occur. Underlying it all is the fact that this is largely when the astrological year kicks it up a notch in in intensity. Things start to happen. Energetic patterns start to break loose and change, and overall themes of the year are established.

The Power of Reflection

Excerpt from an article originally published in the *Dolmen Grove Chronicles* in The Lockdown Issue, 2020.

A lot of people are spending a lot of time alone right now, and one of the most powerful things you can do is to turn your attention inward in the name of personal reflection and growth. However, and this is the important part, right now, it is more or less enforced through wise choices by people who are looking at the best for everyone.

Here's the catch; even when freedom of movement goes back to normal, it will still be a time of reflection and inner work. So, if you thought all of this personal work will stop when freedom of movement is restored, think again.

Nothing could be further from the truth. Why, do you ask? The reason, as with many things, is astrological.

In the middle of May, the two most beneficial planets in astrology will retrograde. Venus and Jupiter both retrograde May 13th.

When planets retrograde, it is a great time to go inward and make the appropriate changes in the name of your personal growth.
The difference between then and now is that theoretically, this reflection will be by choice. After this period, you might choose not to do the appropriate work for the sake of not burning out from the amount of personal work currently being done. However, that is exactly why your work should continue during that retrograde period. If you do maximize your gain during that retrograde period, you will be fantastically set up for a stellar 2021.

This is all broad information. Let's break down the individual planets, so you know where to focus your energy.

Let's start with Venus, which will retrograde from May 13th until June 25th, in the sign of Gemini. In context, this is the shorter of the two. Venus is known as the Lesser Benefic and is generally considered the second most beneficial planet looked at astrologically.

It corresponds to love, beauty, art, creativity, creative expression, the appreciation of all of those things, the manifested goddess, and money. It is also the planet of jealousy, and all things associated with a woman scorned. It is the ruling planet of Taurus and Libra. Since it is retrograding in Gemini, we do see elemental compatibility, since both Gemini and Libra are air signs. This means the retrograde period will be more dynamic than normal.

When Venus is retrograde, the dominant theme is an inward reflection and work involves reassessing your inner femininity. That might be a bitter pill for toxic masculine people to swallow, but that doesn't make it untrue. However, that line of thinking, re-evaluation and the like, can also be applied to your own creativity. During this retrograde, re-evaluating your creativity could be just as helpful and effective as taking a second look at your inner sexuality, specifically your feminine side and how you express it.

The Gemini influence tells us the main vessel for this will be personal communication, whether through the personal computer, telephone, or brief conversations with a variety of people. Also of note is that many times during a Venus retrograde, exes and people from your past may come back into your life.

Here again, the Gemini influence tells us this may be short-lived.

Jupiter, the Greater Benefic, will retrograde from May 13th until September 13th, in the sign of Capricorn so that this duration will be significantly longer. However, that also means the intensity will not be as intense as it is during the Venus retrograde. And exes and other people from your past are generally not going to come back during this time, so rest easy knowing that.

There are some other traits to take the edge off of things, too, so let's take a closer look. Jupiter corresponds to prosperity, the expansion of consciousness, living extravagantly, rulership, spirituality, large living spaces, philosophy, good fortune, and leaders, to name a few. It is the ruling planet of Sagittarius and a co-ruling planet of Pisces, so we see it aligns with fire and water energy. Jupiter retrograde also occupies a special place in astrology. Due to its size and beneficial nature, it is generally considered that when Jupiter is retrograde, it is not *that* much different than when it is direct.

There is still one major characteristic of Jupiter retrograde, which is that generally, it denotes there is a duality of some sort present.

For example, if Jupiter is retrograde in a natal chart, it can mean someone came from a divorced household. Or perhaps was raised in the city and spent their summers in the country.

Whichever way it plays out, it is simply worth noting there is a duality of some kind present.

When it comes to the transiting (daily) sky, this takes on a very different nature. On the one hand, this could mean that there is a duplicity of some sort occurring. For example, think of the symbolism of duck medicine.
In Native American traditions, working with animal symbolism and energies is known as medicine.

Apropos, no? On the surface of the water, the duck looks like it isn't doing anything to move across the surface of the water, but under the surface, those webbed feet are paddling a million miles an hour. On the other hand, this serves as a warning that during this time, things may not be as they appear. It also means that now is a great time to get a lot of things done behind the scenes while everyone is preoccupied with other matters. In any event, your inner life can be addressed right now, continuing your process of growth.

Now that you know this information, you can see what I mean by the opportunities present throughout September to continue your inner growth. The height of this only lasts until late June when Venus goes direct, then it will continue more gently through September.

If you know you are going to be tired of internal work by mid-May, when Venus retrogrades, then I am the bearer of bad news, because you may be done with it but it is not done with you, so it will be brought to your door until Venus stops dancing. Even then, Jupiter continues to linger in the background until mid-September, telling us there is more to the story than you see.

The light at the end of the tunnel is that both of these planets will be direct just in time for the holidays and the beginning of 2021, which sets the stage for a great start.

And another piece of good news is that Venus only retrogrades about every two years, so you won't have to worry about those people from your past coming back up every year, only when you are starting to forget about them and move on.

Samhain

Now we come to arguably the most popular and influential sabbat, Samhain. It is influential because it evolved to create the modern-day Halloween. Some say that Halloween and Samhain are the same thing. Technically that is not accurate but liberally, it is. In this way it is a paradox. Samhain is an ancient Gaelic festival historically celebrated on November first. Like other fire festivals it starts the night before at sundown, which is why it is celebrated the evening of October 31st rather than November 1st.

Samhain marks the final harvest of the year and the beginning of the dark months. The common belief is that it is the when the veil between the worlds is the thinnest.
A lesser-known fact is that there is another time when the veil between the worlds is the thinnest, and that is Beltane, the opposite festival. I have written about this before, pointing out the symmetry and metaphysics involved in this, and in short, just like there are two festivals when the veil between the worlds is the thinnest, there are also times when the veil between the worlds is the thickest, a scientific point many ignore. Because of the thin veil, spirit contact, especially with ancestors, is a characteristic practice of this festival.

This was also a festival of sacrifice, both animal and human, as well as ritualistic slaughter. Divination is also a feature of this festival, as is the wearing of masks. The reason for the masks is open to dispute, but it is generally accepted that people wore masks to blend in with the other spirits that appear during this time. Hence, we have the source for modern Halloween costumes.

In a dark twist, the sacrifices that were made at this time were to ensure a successful winter, whereas sacrifices earlier in the year were to ensure a successful planting. This gives further insight into this holiday, with it being more focused around animals than the other festivals, and some believe this means that the roots of this festival are more in line with animal husbandry rather than agriculture.

This puts it in stark contrast to the other fire festivals that have to do with the first sprouting of plants, etc.

Another interesting trait of this festival is that of faery contact. To my knowledge, few, if any, festivals mention the fae specifically, but this is not the case with Samhain.

Technically, Samhain is a festival during which it is easier than normal to communicate with faeries.

In many cultures, this was also a time of administration. Rulers would make decrees and banishments during this festival, and heroes made heroic stands against monsters, too. As has been said before, Beltane is a festival of life and Samhain, its opposite, is a festival of death.

Even though Samhain is seen as the beginning of winter, it was also seen as the beginning of the next calendar year. These points are inconsistently found, so this is open to interpretation, I mention it here because many people today claim that Samhain is the beginning of the upcoming year.

If you follow this line of thinking, you arrive at the conclusion that this is the first fire festival of the year, which of course flies in the face of our modern calendar.

Remembering that Samhain is a festival of the dead, I find it highly interesting that the new year starts off focused on death rather than life. We can say this is still true today in the northern hemisphere, since January starts in the middle of winter.

There are many alternative names for this festival, and a lot of them are related, for example, Samhain, Sauin, and Oiche Shamhna.

There are other names that are distinct, such as All Hallow's Eve, All Hallows, and in other parts of the world, Día de los Muertos. Christianity calls it All Saints Day, and immediately follows it with All Souls Day.

Earlier I pointed out that the root of the wheel of the year is Eurocentric and specifically from the British Isles and some parts of northern Europe, and I circle back to this thought because I have a homework assignment. For those of you that have seen me present or taken one of my classes, you know how much I love giving homework!

I encourage you to investigate when festivals in your area and spiritual paradigm have traditionally been held that honor the dead and the connection with the invisible world. Many cultures have days and festivals of the dead with long-standing traditions, so there is quite the variety of practices, and those are just the ones that have survived the test of time.

In a lot of ways, Samhain is more than just a festival to honor the dead. In a broad and accurate sense, as mentioned above, Samhain is a festival to work with beings that live in the spiritual realm, whether they are dead to us or simply etheric beings. I point this out because you can contact more than just the dead or ancestors, but this point is neglected in common parlance. This makes Samhain a festival that is more along the lines of a spirit contact event rather than necromantic. Working with the fae, divination, and strengthening your connection with spirit guides and teachers can all be appropriate subjects during this time.

As an extension of this, I find it humorous that it is considered a 'witchy' holiday, because that is technically inaccurate. That is what Hexennacht is for, and Samhain is more based on connecting with the invisible world in general. I know many people who are not witches who work with Samhain energy to connect with deceased ancestors. Samhain is an excellent time to get in touch with your lineage, whether it is making peace with deceased relatives, discovering information they have to share with you, or revealing spiritual gifts you might otherwise not know you have.

As Leonardo da Vinci pointed out in his journals, alchemy and necromancy are two sides of the same coin (to paraphrase), so if you consider Beltane a festival of life, then Samhain is a festival of death, and you can't have one without the other.

This also means if you're going to celebrate one, you should celebrate the other, too. There's no reason to be an unbalanced spirit, after all.

A warning should be given here; when you deal with the fae, you should be very careful. This is a point that is highly controversial today, although historically accurate. If you look at the history of the relationship between humans and the fae folk, you see that more often than not, it has been a contentious relationship. By and large they have no love for humanity, and usually with good reason. Unlike what modern fairytales would have us believe, they are not harmless, nor are they generally disposed to having good relations with us. A lot of this has to do with the person who seeks to contact them, although healthy relations with the fae are more the exception to the rule than the rule itself. More often than not, the fae are antagonistic to humans and human interaction. This does not mean you cannot have good relations with them, rather that it is wise to know the stories and tread lightly when dealing with them. And above all, do not be antagonistic to them.

I have worked with fae folk extensively throughout the years and when I was young and inexperienced those relations didn't go well.

The more I grew as a person, the better the interactions became. I don't let my guard down though, and I have the feeling they don't, either.

This warning points to a larger problem not discussed in books, which is the relationship between disincarnate spirits and humans. For the last two-thousand years, humanity has largely interacted in a toxic way to them. If you look at the bulk of work in the Western Esoteric Tradition, you find a reoccurring theme. That theme is the mindset of the practitioner, which is to say to the spirit "do this (what is asked) or God will punish you."

There are groups of people who are the exception to this approach, although on average, this is how things have transpired. It is only within the last few decades that we as a species have evolved to the point that this is changing. However, spirits on the other side of the veil are still shell-shocked from two thousand years of abuse, so they are slow in some cases to change their attitudes toward us. When dealing with spirits, it is wise to keep this in mind.

Just because you have a healthy mindset about interacting with them doesn't mean they have forgiven us (the human species), so it is on us to treat them with respect and understand where their headspace is at.

This should also be tempered with the fact that they have long memories and agendas that are alien to us, so we should not presume to know their psyches.

I don't intend for this information to scare you, rather to give you words of caution to keep in mind when it comes to dealing with them. Most of the spirits I have worked with over the last thirty-five plus years have been amenable if I have been, so more often not your relations with them will go fine, but if you ever encounter a particularly malicious or stand-offish spirit, now you see why.

They cannot be blamed for this, and the responsibility is on us to do our Will while repairing the damage done during the dominance of the Abrahamic religions.

All of this should be kept in mind in general, especially when it comes to Samhain. In a lot of ways, Samhain is a dark trickster holiday which is evidenced by mask wearing, so if there is ever a time a spirit will be malicious, this is it. Entire books have been written on Samhain, so I will wrap up here. Just know that as much as has been written about Samhain, there is just as much of the festival that is experiential, so until you have experienced Samhain, you will only have half of the story.

I encourage you to explore further in line with your spiritual paradigm, and also to not be afraid. Intention and purity can go a long way when it comes to achieving success in your spirit work, and there is no better time to start than Samhain.

CHAPTER SEVEN
MIDSUMMER/MIDWINTER

Even though I touched on the solstices and equinoxes earlier, I want to come back to the festivals associated with them now. We will skip the energetic side of them and will rather focus on the festivals themselves.

This festival axis is based on the idea of extremes. That is something normal to the human condition – being prone to extremes. Celebrated on these days are extreme light and extreme dark, extreme heat and extreme cold. With these extremes come the promise of equilibrium. In a roundabout way, the point of these festivals is to encourage the practitioner to find equilibrium within, or to bring something in their lives into equilibrium.

A good example of this would be finding the balance between work and play, responsibilities and irresponsibilities, or whatever polarity you can conceive.

These days are when the most or least amount of sun is present, and like all other festivals, they are opposite in the hemispheres.

The June solstice is the summer solstice in the northern hemisphere, and it is the winter solstice in the southern. The December solstice is winter solstice in the northern hemisphere and summer solstice in the southern.

When you shift your perspective, you find lack is present, too. For example, the summer solstice is the time of maximum light and also the biggest lack of darkness, and the winter solstice is the time of maximum darkness and also the lack of light. While these may seem like pedantic points, they can be quite useful when designing your festival activities.

Do you decide to focus on what is present, or what is absent? This largely depends on your intent, don't forget that the verbiage you use is how your subconscious will be programmed, and your environment at large.

Neither of these festivals have to do with finding balance, either in yourself or your life. That is the role of the equinoxes. You may see where you need equilibrium in your life but these are not the times to put it into practice, at least not yet. Simply identifying these subjects is enough for now. Also of note is that neither of these have to do with planting seeds. By the time of the solstice, the seeds have been planted, nurtured, and are coming to fruition.

Gratitude is a trait that is associated with winter solstice, but not summer, and creativity is associated with summer solstice but not winter, so we find that as much as these two festivals are parallel, they are also strikingly different.

Another point that is quite fun, yet deviant in thought, is that both of these are extremes, so you can embrace the extremes they present.

The best example of this is summer solstice which is a time during which many people focus their intents on shining the best and brightest in their lives. This is why it is wise to roll out new projects that put you in the spotlight in one way or another. This is also why many couples decide to get married around this time. Romantically, they are shining their best and brightest.

This also means that winter solstice is a time of extreme darkness or of extreme lack. This can be helpful to keep in mind when facing situations that have to be decreased, or when it is necessary to move in shadows and darkness. Here are a couple of examples to illustrate the point. If you want to break a bad habit, this is the time to do it because you are focusing on decreasing its power over you.

This same line of thought can be used if you choose to deal with an addiction. Now is the time when it is at its weakest.

The phrase 'moving in shadows and darkness' requires a bit of an explanation. A good rule of thumb throughout life is to not let people know what you are doing until you have done it, or it is too late for anyone to do anything about it. The word 'darkness' can also be taken literally, meaning this is a good time to work with darker entities if that is part of your spiritual paradigm.

Summer Solstice

Summer solstice, also known as Midsummer or Litha, is celebrated when the daylight is at its maximum, and the sun is at the highest point in the sky. Since light and heat are at their strongest, you can tell that the sun is the principal catalyst. Projects begun at this time are ones that put you in a position to shine your best and brightest. Purification through fire is another theme, as is the destructive nature of fire. The same sun that makes things grow can also start a wildfire. This hints at activities that are done during this festival such as power, activity, energy, and harnessing the divine fire accessible to all.

Not everything is sunshine and roses, and there are more controversial traits of summer solstice festivities. Other activities associated with this festival include battle, conflict, and competition. These characteristics have different perspectives associated with them, so we cannot lump them all together, nor treat them the same.

The first perspective is that of competition, conflict, and battle just for the sake of it. Some people simply enjoy the thrill of the fight, so to speak, and this is the festival for them. The second perspective is, temperatures are elevated, so people have shorter tempers, meaning that some of these traits can come into being more than during other festivals or times of the year. The third perspective is a more abstract one which focuses on the battle – the battle between light and dark, growth and entropy.

While this is the time of maximum light and heat, it is also the beginning of the end, the beginning of the rise of darkness and decay. Historically the stories associated with this have to do with the battle of the king of light and the king of darkness, symbolized in various cultures by many terms and stories. Up until now the days have been getting longer, but now darkness starts to rise, and this transition is not always a preferred one, nor an easy one.

As much as people like to hold onto the light and heat, darkness and cold is inevitable.

This is the eternal interplay of growth and decay, light and dark, life and death. After all, the only constant is change.

One of the ways this struggle has been portrayed is through traditional witchcraft ideas like the Oak King and Holly King. During the waxing part of the year, that which reaches its zenith on summer solstice, the Oak King is in power, and this changes through a battle with his opposition, the Holly King.

Much has been written about this in traditional witchcraft books, so I won't go deeply into it here. It is worth noting because it gives us an example of the energetics of this holiday.

There are various activities that are appropriate to this festival, and some of them overlap with the following festival of Lughnasadh. This includes such activities as feats of strength, competitive games, and exhibitions of prowess. Bonfires are also part of this festival, as you might expect, and arguably, the bigger the better. When it comes to herbs and plants associated with this festival, fennel and sorghum stalks are commonly found representing the light and the dark, respectively.

As a matter of fact, we find an interesting connection when it comes to fennel, because legend has it that Prometheus smuggled a tongue of flame out of the realm of the gods in a fennel shaft so that humanity would have fire. Thus, the story of Prometheus is an appropriate story for this festival.

Technically, any and all solar deities align with this festival, but Prometheus is worth singling out because of the fennel connection.

When designing rituals and ceremonies for this festival keep these qualities in mind and you will have no problem generating something powerful and personal. This means this is also a good festival for confronting and dealing with your inner darkness. After all, during this time it is minimized, making it easier to work with and address.

In a lot of ways, this festival can be comparable to a full moon, and its counterpart, the winter solstice, a new moon. This is a broad idea, but I'm sure you see my meaning. Then, by extension, the festivals in between can be seen as parallel to quarter moons. I simply point out these observations here to demonstrate the accuracy of the Hermetic axiom, As Above, So Below.

Nothing is perfect nor lasts forever, which sets the stage for the counterpart festival of winter solstice.

Winter Solstice

Winter solstice, also known as Yule, also known as Midwinter, is the counterpart festival to the summer solstice. In the northern hemisphere it is celebrated in late December, whereas in the southern it is celebrated in late June. While it is celebrated as the beginning of the season, we know it is really the apex. Following the line of thought through from above, we realize this is the longest night of the year, the time of greatest darkness and also the time of least light. Effectively, this makes it the coldest time of the year as well, or at least the beginning of the cold times.

The main theme is that of nurturing the light during times of darkness and cold. In previous times it was a challenge to keep the hearth fire going during the long winter months. Let's think about this for a moment. If you hadn't made the right provisions, you and yours could be facing starvation or freezing to death during winter. Hence, this festival is one of nurturing the light, both symbolically and physically, while at the same time recognizing that the light is at its weakest, meaning it is harder than normal to nurture and foster. All of these traits make it a bleak holiday in comparison to the earlier, happier ones of Ostara, Beltane, and Midsummer.

Winter solstice immediately follows Samhain, and whereas Samhain was the gateway to the dark times, winter solstice is THE dark time. The veil between the worlds is not as thin here as it is during Beltane or Samhain – like summer solstice, it is much thicker. This means this festival is not as much about spirit contact as it is the cold hard facts of life and soul. Winter solstice is truly the festival of the dead, not in regards to ancestors or necromancy, rather lifelessness. In a lot of ways, this holiday is a litmus test. We are no longer at the point of evaluation or inventory, we are at the point of using what is present or acknowledging how our lack limits us. This can be a particularly painful revelation to some, especially if it occurs when all is dead and cold.

Psychospiritually, this is a good time to work with the shadow self, as darkness can correspond to the unknown within our subconscious and bring what is hidden in the darkness into the light of day. Techniques like hypnosis, shamanic journeying, and other practices can be particularly effective if done during this time.

The shadow-self is not only the receptacle of bad habits and addictions, it is also where we find ignorance, insecurities, and other psychological wounds that have occurred in life. The treasure in this underworld is intuition and tapping into potential you didn't know existed.

While working with the subconscious, beware, do not try and get rid of it. Everything casts a shadow, and therefore it is better to make your darkness visible and bring it under your control than it is to foolishly try to get rid of it. Controlling and developing your shadow is a much better goal and approach than trying to eliminate it entirely, and more rewarding, at that.

While it may seem that all is lost, that is most emphatically not the case. It is in the darkness of the womb that life is nurtured. It is in darkness that the seed incubates and eventually grows.

This line of reasoning leads us to a very important part of winter solstice, which is that this festival is the birth of the sun god. He does not immediately grow into adulthood, rather his story begins here and develops now until summer solstice, six months away. I have always found this point interesting because it was this inspiration that laid the foundation for

Christianity and its myth of Jesus the Christ being born in late December. Christians used the date of December 25th, but we know the actual date they align with is the winter solstice in the northern hemisphere. There are various reasons why they chose the 25th instead of solstice, however, that is a conversation for another time. Suffice to know for now that Christianity is continuing Pagan practices long observed before the rise of their own belief system.

This is the festival that sees the birth of the sun god, not the fully realized or formed sun god. In a roundabout way, this means this is the ending of the cycle of the pregnant goddess who will now blossom into motherhood. We should be mindful of the vulnerability of the sun god and the protective nature and qualities of the mother goddess.

I find this interesting to consider because if you look at the majority of archaeological finds, the oldest are those of goddess figures when it comes to representations of deities. Putting it bluntly, statuary of the goddess predates statuary of the god by thousands of years. While this does not prove the archaic erroneous claims of a matriarchal world religion, it does remind us that the earliest roots of our species saw the value and importance of woman, and therefore the goddess.

There are the occasional extremist sects that claim images of a god predate all or most depictions of a goddess, but these are paper-thin arguments that don't hold up to the light of reasoned scrutiny.

In modern times, this festival is celebrated in the name of family and the home. Drawing close to loved ones and taking comfort and pleasure in these close ties is a major part of midwinter as it is practiced today, and in this way, it has taken on strong parallels to Christmas.

More accurately, this is a festival of the dark night of the soul. Have you ever been in a period during your life when everything looked hopeless? Where there was no light of hope, no pot of gold at the end of the rainbow, nothing to look forward to the next day? Where there was no reason for continuing?

If you have been there, like so many of us have, then you know what I mean. This is known as the dark night of the soul. It symbolizes when you are lost, confused, frustrated, and feeling hopeless. Dr. Carl Jung writes about this extensively, and much has been made about this idea in common parlance, so I see no reason to readdress it here. I simply mention it for now because it aligns with this festival.

A sublime meaning of this holy day is that of finding the light to go on when all else is lost. This point is usually diluted down to finding warmth in winter, but as you can see, it is much deeper than that.

When it comes to common practices there are several correspondences to note. The first one is that of the Yule log. This is a log that is burned to represent fostering the light even in the darkest of times.

The light in the log also represents the flame of divinity and serves as a reminder that no matter how dark things get, the light of divinity is always present. Another practice associated with midwinter is the Yule boar. This is a boar that is sacrificed in the name of celebration, during which vows are decreed. There are several other correspondences to this festival worth mentioning, and they are all plants that are used in various ways.

The first one to mention is holly, which brings with it visions of holly boughs. The next one on our list is one that is common knowledge as well, and that is mistletoe. Kissing under the mistletoe is one way it has endured and adapted over the centuries.

The other two main plants of winter solstice, pine and ivy, require a little more explanation.

When burned during Yule, pine represents healing, cleansing, and protection, while ivy represents the goddess and the life, death, rebirth process.

Below is an article I wrote that gives insight into what to expect around the time of winter solstice each year.

Astrologically, a lot of the activity we experience is in the final stages of the zodiacal wheel, and because of this, we know what to expect, like clockwork, every year.

Wrap Up and Move On

Excerpt from an article originally published in the *Clan Dolmen Chronicles* in the Spring, 2021 issue.

With the exception of a few fast-moving planets in Gemini, most of the zodiac activity is found in the late signs, Capricorn, Aquarius, and Pisces. Uranus in Taurus is another exception, too, and it will be there for a while. As we move through the sign of Aries, some of Pisces' placements will progress, too. This happens every year by-and-large, although this year there is a little more activity in these signs than average.

All told, there are six chart points in signs before the first sign of Aries and six chart points in signs from Aries forward. This means that until the sun moves into Taurus, energetically speaking, we will have one foot in the past and one in the present. This is very liberating in that it permits us to readdress some things we might not have finished with yet and come back to our present and future projects on our own timetable.

In a lot of ways, this is a microcosmic look at a macrocosmic subject. Because of recent events such as the epidemic and significant political occurrences in various countries, we can see that the macro to this situation is that most of the world is in some sort of transitional period, between the old and the new.

Those of you who read the last issue's article know that a lot of this ties into the Great Conjunction that will influence things over the next year. This point is worth knowing because it gives us context.

The problem presented here is that to transcend, one must take risks and leaps of faith into the unknown, which our species has always struggled with. We can justify stepping back and looking at where we have come from and what is left to be done because of what is happening astrologically.

Two years from now will be when we can move fully forward. Until then, various parts of the past will be there to be addressed.

This year these subjects have to do with the mental plane and the element of air. Next year the theme will be on the emotional leftovers. The Aries ingress of 2023 will be all about new beginnings and pioneering into unknown territories. Of course, we can do that before then, but it is then that the stars support us more fully.

In a broad sense, this year's theme is that of evaluating and changing social interactions and redefining one's place within the greater planetary context and scheme of things. There is a technique in astrology called midpoints.

This can be very useful for deciding how to respond to what is going on astrologically and how to develop self-empowerment.

If you look at the range of planets as of the March equinox – the range from late Capricorn (Pluto) to the middle of Gemini (the moon) – this puts the midpoint at eleven degrees Aries. There is a planet located near there, Chiron, the planet of the wounded and the healer. In Aries, Chiron tells us that there is a wounded sense of being or sense of self that may be prevalent right now. If you have that placement in your natal chart, the house position tells you what that sense of being is connected to, if you don't, you can still learn about this by looking at the world around you.

There is a lot happening right now that has to do with people reclaiming their power, or people who never had their power who are now finding their voice. This is the clearest example of Chiron in Aries that we can see because it is happening outside of ourselves, making it more visible.

There is another part of this; right now, there are a lot of wounded people out there who think they are reclaiming their power, in reality, they are blinded by their privilege. While that could be an essay in and of itself, I will not go in-depth on it here.

Wounds are coming to the surface and being exposed. Some of these wounds are new, while others are merely being seen for the first time.

Before we can individually and collectively move on, it would be wise to do internal healing. The best way to perform the initial assessment is through self-reflection, using society's greater whole as your context.

Once this assessment has been done, you can formulate a plan, and given what we discussed before, you can see that this plan is partial cleanup, partial preparation, and partial implementation. Three points of a trident, if you will. Because of all of this, you can see how I really can't say much more on this subject at this time because what I reference is highly subjective and personal.

Recalling the Great Conjunction, we can see that there is good news that goes along with this. This conjunction usually smiles favorably on the people of the time in some way or another.

This doesn't mean everything comes up roses, rather this underscores the power of this time. In the tarot, the astrological sign of Aquarius corresponds to Major Arcana card seventeen, The Star. This card usually corresponds to the stars lining up, blessings coming forth, and all things beneficial.

Whenever you get frustrated, depressed, or in some other way thrown out of sorts this year, reflect on The Star. Perhaps what you are going through is a backhanded compliment. Or perhaps what you are dealing with is what is necessary to prepare you for what is to come.

Even though a lot of this has to do with the Great Conjunction, there is a lot that also has to do with, well, you. Have you stopped and reassessed where you are versus where you were a few years ago? What are your plans for the year? Any of them you begin now will have the extra energy of the zodiacal year behind them, fueling your progress. What is still undone that needs to be taken care of before you can move forward? The Mercury retrogrades this year will happen in air signs, meaning whatever needs to be done will be brought to the surface, so don't worry if you miss something now. It will be brought up to you later, whether you want it to or not. Patience is critical here, as is discipline.

Remember that the seeds you sow here will blossom later this year, and depending on how big your plans are, they may take even longer to manifest – with diligence, they will manifest. With the primary focus right now on Aquarius and Pisces, the environment is ripe for the visionary and progressive. To paraphrase Albert Einstein, we will not solve our problems with the same thinking that was present when they were created.

I wonder, will we collectively step up and actualize this? If so, it will happen either this year or years from now; we will look back and see how critical the year 2021 was.

So, knowing this, where do you stand? What is your agenda? How will you use your healing to create positive and lasting growth? And most importantly, when that is done, how will you help others?

APPENDIX I
NUIT

Underlying all of these observances about the wheel of the year is something we have not yet discussed, which is the Milky Way. That thick band of stars that runs across the sky, which is particularly visible in the black sky of night. Before we get to that, there are a few other things to note. First, the name of our galaxy is the Milky Way, and when we are looking at that silver band, we are looking towards the center of our galaxy, which is currently located at twenty-seven degrees Sagittarius, astrologically speaking. If you are astrologically literate, check to see if you have anything in your chart at that degree because if you do, you have a connection with our macrocosm.

Technically, Earth is located on one of the spiral arms of the Milky Way, nowhere near the center, and since we haven't developed the technology nor ability to visit that area of space, we are left with deductions and speculation as to what it is like there. Of course, many theories, some wild, some sensical, have been created over the years and if you ever get bored, it is entertaining and worth the research.

I am not going to address them here because I want to focus on something more magical, which is the goddess that is the Milky Way and so much more; the Egyptian goddess Nu(i)t.

She is the axle of the year. All seasonal festivals spin around her central core. She is the sky, and she has been with us since the beginning. Even if you remove her ancient Egyptian façade, you come to realize that the night sky has been with us as long as there has been a planet Earth, even before the rise of homo sapiens. When you are standing on the Earth's surface at night, she occupies half of what we know as reality. As long as sentient life has existed, she has been there watching.

Ancient Egyptians noticed her connection with Earth, as is evidenced by the fact that she is the cosmic reflection of the river Nile, and I don't mean that in a symbolic way. If you are standing in or floating on the middle of the Nile and look up, you will see that she runs in the same direction across the sky as the river itself. This led the ancient Egyptians to believe that the Milky Way was the cosmic river, the non-physical counterpart to the Nile.

Nut, or Nuit as she is commonly called today, has the roots of her name in ancient Egypt, but many other ancient cultures had a sky goddess.

Although she was not specifically called a night sky goddess, rather various other terms such as the void, or the state of nothingness that existed before somethingness came into being.

In ancient Egyptian theology, she was the counterpart to Geb, the Earth god, and in this way the two formed the whole of what we can see and experience. Not only were they paramours, they were also brother and sister, and through their union, other gods came into being. We see their union every night when we step outside and stargaze. Our feet are firmly planted on Geb, and everything we need and use comes from him, but our mind is drawn to Nuit, usually because of her mysteries.

That's the thing about her, she is the great mystery. Until such time that we explore the stars and find out for ourselves, she is the unknown and the unknowable. Who knows what we will find when we explore her ad nauseum? We can speculate, infer, and deduce all we want, but until we chart the stars, we simply will not know.

On the one hand, this is fantastic because it gives us freedom to dream and fantasize, on the other, this is intimidating because she is so expansive and beyond comprehension that we may feel miniscule in comparison.

One thing we should remember is that all of our science and physics, both quantum and meta, are geocentric, and it would be a sin of pride to think that they hold true in space like they do here.

To begin to know her, we first have to start with her name: Nuit. In ancient Egypt she was known as Nut (pronounced 'newt'). The ancient Egyptian language didn't use vowels, so we are left with deductions and speculations as to how it was spoken, and Nut is the closest we have determined at this time. The change in her name from Nut to Nuit is nothing formal, rather it is a byproduct of modern occultism and occulture. It was the British magician, Aleister Crowley, who popularized this spelling of her name and promulgated it through his philosophy of Thelema. One of the reasons he chose that spelling is because the word nuit is French for night, so by adjusting the spelling, he was also showing his cheeky wit. In modern times her name is spelled either way, and the further we go into this century, the less people care how it is spelled because at the end of the day it is the same goddess.

Nuit and her consort Geb are children of Shu and Tefnut. Shu is the god of air and the wind, and Tefnut is the goddess of moist air, dew, and rain.

You can see that this is a very basic understanding of the condensation process: air plus moisture equals water.

The water eventually becomes a breeding place for the inevitable formation of land, Geb, which in turn will eventually evolve into a land mass, and from there, life will grow if circumstances are right. Is this a watered-down story the ancient Egyptians passed along that had to do with long-forgotten knowledge?

Or is it a symbolic story trying to understand how everything came into being? The latter is commonly accepted today, and that is canon, but we cannot rule out the possibility that it is literal, too.

In turn, Nuit and Geb birthed the famous five: Set, Nephthys, Isis, Osiris, and in some stories, Horus. The genealogy we're discussing is simply one tale, and in other areas of ancient Egypt, other tales were told.

I point this out because, thanks to the sands of time, most of the stories and traditions of ancient Egypt are no longer with us, and all we have are our best put together theories based on what we do know.

Considering that the ancient Egyptian empire lasted three thousand years, we are left with the very reasonable thought that if we can imagine a story, it probably existed during that time. I am using this genealogy because we can see a further extrapolation on the aforementioned themes.

Earth (Geb) and sky (Nuit) gave birth to the initiation principle (Set), the life principle (Osiris), the goddess principle (shown as a duality – Isis, the visible goddess of life, and Nephthys, the invisible goddess of death), and the principle of exploration and conquest (Horus).

Looking at these deities as symbolic is in line with how Nuit is perceived today. She is the goddess of the sky, especially strong at night, and the goddess of stars, the cosmos, astronomy, mothers, and ultimately the universe. In modern occult circles, especially those influenced by Thelema, she symbolically represents the principle of expansion, whether it is the expansion of consciousness, finances, or the waistline.

In this way we see a strong parallel to the Hindu god Shiva, which includes a major drawback, which is 'too much of a good thing'.

It is possible to expand too much, and the tempering phrase from Edward Abbey: "Growth for the sake of growth is the ideology of the cancer cell." There is such a thing as expanding too much, to the point where the mind pops like an overinflated balloon.

Some of you may disagree with this, but physiologically and psychologically there are limits to how much we can expand before we mentally break.

This is often diagnosed and dissected in psychological circles, and I leave it to you to inquire in that field for further information on mental breaks.

Also, in Thelema, her counterpart is not Geb, rather it is Hadit, who represents the principle of contraction, the sacred center and core that exists in everything. Through their interplay, an eternal dance of expansion and contraction occur, which we can witness if we study our breath.

When I first learned Thelema, I had already been studying ancient Egypt for about fifteen years and therefore knew the connection between Nuit and Geb, so the shift to being paired with Hadit in Thelema did not sit right with me.

I asked a dear friend and mentor of mine about it, and she responded that this shift from ancient Egyptian thought to that notion within Thelema simply shows a shift in focus to a greater paradigm, and those words have stayed with me and influenced me since I first heard them many years ago.

In Egyptian iconography, Nuit is usually depicted as an arching female body over the ground below. Her body is full of stars, obviously reminiscent of the Milky Way itself.

This pose is usually seen as a protective gesture, protecting the Earth and all things on it from what lies beyond her. This infers that there are dangers in deep space that can threaten our existence, things from beyond, and since she corresponds to the galaxy and the cosmos, we can also deduce that these potential threats originate from either another dimension or a source far beyond our comprehension.

I find this an interesting point because it is not talked about much, if at all, but it is logically plausible. This also extends the line of thought I just mentioned – that the ancient Egyptians knew about things from beyond our comprehension and potentially beyond our reality.

Part of her role was also to swallow the sun when it set every night, only to give birth to it the next morning. In essence this was the beginning of understanding the cycles of the sun and the moon. Another part of her role was that of a proto-Charon type character, in that she was the one who ferried souls away from Earth once they died. I say 'away from Earth' rather than naming a particular destination because we really don't know where they were ultimately headed.

Tradition tells us that if we look at the alignment of sacred Egyptian sites and the stars, we find that they do line up with certain stars, and if we take into account that she was simply the road they traveled, they could have gone beyond what we know of as the cosmos.

This is congruent with ancient Egyptian thought, because it was believed the souls went to an invisible place, an afterlife, to use a modern concept. More specifically she could be seen as the path of the soul itself rather than a sentient being that guides them.

Ancient Egyptians understood a scientific principle that went undiscussed and undiscovered for millennia after their empire fell, which is that there is an invisible side to everything that is visible.

While we know it as a Newtonian principle, they knew it as the *duat*. The concept of the duat has been erroneously attributed to meaning the underworld exclusively, in reality, it simply means duality. So, when we see references to the duat in Egyptian texts, we should not think of the afterlife, rather simply journeying into the nonphysical.

While this may seem tangential to our overall theme in the book, it is actually a lynch pin, because when we look at the wheel of the year, we should remember that 1) to know a festival, it is wise to study it's opposite, and 2) everything that we see and experience has an invisible component. We can use this information when planning rituals and also when learning what is metaphysically happening at each festival. And all of this is thanks to Nuit.

Book of Nut

Let's take a closer look at Nuit through a text attributed to, or dedicated to her, and that is a lesser-known Egyptian text commonly known as *Book of Nut*, and before that, *The Fundamentals of the Course of the Stars*. It is not a book as we would think of it today, it is a collection of papyri that discusses astronomical and mythological topics.

While it is an ancient Egyptian tome, it is not that old, comparatively speaking, and roughly dates back to the 26th dynasty, as the empire was on its way out. I mention this because it is not that ancient of a text, so it is likely that many foreign ideas influenced it and is thus not a solely Egyptian stream of thought.

In this work, cycles of the sun, moon, planets, and important stars to the Egyptians are discussed. Additionally, the tools of the art are discussed as well, which includes sundials and related instruments. It is full of illustrations of Nuit, and sky charts in ancient Egyptian style.

Also contained therein are verses and texts addressing other Egyptian deities like Nekhbet ('She who opens Nuit' is one of her titles), and those that align with Nuit and Egyptian cosmology. Special emphasis is placed on the decans that the sun travels through during the night.

Let's dive a little deeper into this to truly understand the decans. There are two ways this term is used. The first is in its modern context where it describes three, ten-degree divisions of an astrological sign. Each of those divisions are ruled by a planet that rules another sign of the same element.

For example, the first ten degrees of the mutable sign Gemini is ruled by Mercury, because Mercury is the overall ruling planet of the sign. However, the second ten-degree division of Gemini is ruled by Venus, because in the zodiac, Libra is the next air sign after Gemini. So, if you have a planet at twelve degrees Gemini, it is ruled by Mercury and Venus. Then the third ten-degree section is ruled by Saturn or Uranus, depending on when you were born, because both of those are ruling planets of Aquarius, the final of the three air signs in the zodiacal wheel. This formula is applied to all astrological signs and its application can fine tune your interpretation of chart points located there. This is the schema accepted by professional western astrologers today.

This structure is a continuation of ancient Egyptian astrology, and in this way, it is an homage to one of the roots of modern astrology.

In ancient Egypt their month was dictated by the moon and was split into three, ten-day weeks. In ancient Egypt there are thirty-six groups of stars which divide the ecliptic into thirty-six parts of ten degrees each. Another division of time in ancient Egypt is necessary to understand how Egyptians viewed Nuit.

Egyptian theology tells us that once Nuit swallows Ra each night, he traverses the dark underworld on his ship. For an hour duration he occupies one part of the sky and faces trials and attacks associated with their ruler and character. Thus, each of these periods has characteristics and a ruler that Ra, assisted by his crew, must best, usually through combat spearheaded by Set.

The Day

In this context, day does not specify the period during which the sun rules life, rather it is meant to embrace all of the day – the day and the night. There is something to know before we begin. Ancient Egyptians did not recognize midnight as we do today. Practically, this means that the day began at dawn the next day, which is also when the previous day ended. I point this out because the very popular ritual *Liber Resh vel Helios* takes midnight into account, and in this way, it deviates from traditional previous practices.

This is not a knock against that ritual, rather it serves to highlight how a ritual has been adapted to modern times. *Liber Resh*, as it is called, is a much older ritual, however, in the original version, it did not recognize midnight.

Originally it was a three-piece ritual instead of a four, and triangulation and all things related to the number three played important roles during those times, which you saw with the division of the month into three ten-day weeks.

During the day, the sun god Ra traveled the sky as gods are wont to do. The daytime lasted about twelve hours, as did the night. During the day various tools marked time, but during the night the stars lit the way. It was during the night that Ra traveled through Nuit's body. Technically this was the underworld from a certain point of view, as darkness was more absolute than light, and thus the dual side of time.

Ancient Egyptian astronomers noticed certain things about the stars themselves and the patterns they made, and they used these observations to create stories about their deities. These stories were more than the pedestrian question of what happens to the sun at night, or a system of social and political control. These stories conveyed spiritual and religious wisdom that had been passed down for generations and served to preserve and develop the invisible development of the species while the accomplishments of the day served to develop the visible development of the species.

The Night

During later dynasties this wisdom and guidance were collected into a text called *The Book of Gates*. This collection of work looks at the journey of Ra through the underworld at night. It breaks down the night into twelve one-hour blocks of time. Each of these blocks have particular correspondences associated with them, and during them, Ra faced tests that proved his divinity. However, also during these time periods, souls were guided to their eventual destinations, whether divine or cursed. Some say that this is all florid imagery for the soul traveling into outer space, with particular stars as their destinations, but that is a matter for another time. Instead, we will turn our attention to these periods and will look at characteristics and other pieces of information having to do with them.

In true fashion, we are going to give a modern spin on things. After all, as I have said before, "tradition is peer pressure from dead people." (This is the dedication to *Wails of the Wandering Angels*, my introduction to Enochian magick.)

A radically new way to look at this material is to think of the body of Nuit and the parallel to the human body. Just like humans have an energy system, complete with energy vortices we call chakras, so too does the body of Nuit.

Thus, each of these periods are a journey through her body, and you could even go so far as to argue that each transition from one timeframe to another is passing through a chakra of Nuit. For example, when we shift from the first period to the next, that crossing point could be seen as meeting her root chakra. This is all an idea on my part, but I share it here for your amusement and adaptation. Nothing that I'm saying is rooted in tradition, however, it is entirely plausible and workable.

I won't get into a full breakdown of the gates here because this is not a book on Egyptology nor *The Book of Gates* itself, but for those of you who are interested in the topic, I encourage you to check out Josephine McCarthy's book by the same name. It is the most comprehensive book on the subject to date. I mention the gates here for the above reason, and also to let you know that this is where the idea of lunar mansions comes from, another topic tabled for another time. In short, lunar mansions are similar to the hours of the night from ancient Egyptian thought, and the way mansions and gates tie into our working is to let you know that when you are planning a ritual, one of the things you can do is to research your preferred spiritual tradition to see if anything similar exists that you can use for timing purposes.

For example, if you work with the draconian tradition, you could select the hour of the night that corresponds to the serpent. Or, if your timeframe is restricted, you can see what hour of the night you are working with and incorporate the symbolism and imagery into your working. Simply know that the body of Nuit has been micromanaged to this degree and there is ample material available to fine-tune your working in whatever manner you deem appropriate.

I hope all of this information about Nuit helps you see that the night sky has been divided before, and can be done so again, without the need to incorporate midnight.

However, if you do work with the idea of midnight, then remember that the time between midnight and 3 a.m. is commonly known as the Witching Hour. Specifically, 3 a.m. is the exact Witching Hour, but in my youth, I remember the three-hour block of time being just as accurate.

One of my favorite things to do is to execute a ritual between midnight and 3 a.m. on Walpurgisnacht – the Witching Hour on the Witches' Sabbat, if you will.

While these may seem like random thoughts I am sharing, they do have a point, which is that when it comes to timing your festival experiences, feel free to be as creative as you want, and draw from the sources that align with your spiritual paradigm. Do NOT feel like you have to be tied down to one particular thought or approach if it doesn't resonate with you and your path.

APPENDIX II

This is an article I wrote quite some time ago that can give background to Nuit, Aleister Crowley, and Thelema. I realize many of you may not be familiar with these concepts, so I offer this previously published article for those of you who are interested.

Thelema, an Introduction

In 1904, in Cairo, Egypt, Aleister Crowley and his wife Rose received channeled material from three mysterious beings. Three sessions, spread out over three consecutive days, gave rise to the modern spiritual system of Thelema. This material was comprised into *Liber Al vel Legis – The Book of the Law* and became the central holy book for this new spirituality.

Aleister Crowley was a ceremonial magician who studied in the Hermetic Order of the Golden Dawn. He was also well versed in Theosophy and Freemasonry, and these three threads form the foundation of Thelemic beliefs and practices.
While the practices of Thelema are heavily steeped in ceremonial magick, its core beliefs are not as focused.

The central and principal belief of Thelema can be found in its central axiom, 'Do what thou wilt shall be the whole of the law, love is the law, love under will'. In this context, the word will is the will of the higher self, and in that way it also denotes a sense of purpose. At its essence, it tells us that the prime way to live life is through the knowledge and execution of one's purpose, and specifically in a loving fashion.

Beliefs of Thelema include 'every man and every woman is a star', and thus everyone is equal. Living a life where 'existence is pure joy' is another part of the Thelemic code of conduct put forth in *The Book of the Law*.

It also tells us to treat all in a very cautious way, being mindful of the fact that there are those among us that may be disguised advanced souls, and because of that, everyone we meet could be our spiritual equivalent or superior.

However, as Crowley points out, you can have someone living his or her will that has never touched occultism, which further proves his teaching that 'the law is for all'.
From the banker who is doing what they are here to do, all the way to person who is the best parent they can be, because they know it's what they are here to do, Thelema is open to all.

The three central deities in Thelema are the three beings that dictated the verses to Aleister and Rose. They are the ancient Egyptian goddess Nuit, also known as Nut, who is the goddess of expansion and the sky. Hadit, the second being channeled, is the principle of contraction, the sacred point in the circle. Finally, there is Ra-Hoor-Khuit, which is one of the forms of the ancient Egyptian god Horus, and in the case of Thelema, he embodies the principle of expansion and exploration. It is his aeon that is said to be beginning, and thus he is lord of it.

The Thelemic pantheon contains several other beings that will not be mentioned here but have to do with magical and psychological principles. It is in this way that Crowley, through Thelema, advanced the rites and rituals of magick from the old aeon, laying the groundwork for where occultism goes from here, and also, if he has his way, how the human species evolves to its next level.

APPENDIX III

The following article has turned into one of my most popular essay pieces. Not only did I get good feedback on it when it appeared, I have also sent it out many times to people who have asked me about its subject. This in turn has led to people I don't know contacting me from a referral of someone I do know to read it because they are conflicted about its subject matter. I am humbled and amazed by this, and if its popularity continues, I may just turn it into a book. Of course, you can help me determine whether or not I should do this, so ultimately the book's possible publication is in your hands.

So, what is the subject of this article that has been surprisingly popular? Angels. Good, old fashioned angels. I wrote this piece to show that angels are not specifically Judeo-Christian – their roots are much older than that paradigm, and in this essay I have a look at them. I wrote this piece because I, and many like me, have had the same spiritual quandary. Angels are everywhere in the Western Esoteric Tradition, yet if you left the Abrahamic behind, then you might feel like you can't work with them, even though they are so common and influential.

This article is my effort to help you see angels from a different perspective, so that no matter how you choose to work with them, if you choose to work with them at all, you will have knowledge to back up your perspective.

Born of Heat and Light: A look at the pre-Christian roots of angels

Excerpt from an article originally published in the *Dolmen Grove Chronicles* in the Ostara, 2017 issue.

Like so many people in the United States of America, I was born and raised in the Judeo-Christian paradigm of the Abrahamic faiths, Roman Catholicism, to be precise.

Eventually I left that belief system paradigm all together, continuing my path into the occult, and of course, eventually I came to find myself looking at subjects from my Christian days that I had not made peace with yet, and thus I was afforded an opportunity to grow. This was especially true when I discovered the role of angels in the Western Esoteric Tradition, and quickly realized that I should come to peace within myself to clearly work with them.

Of course, it should be clear that I also had to decide whether or not to work with angels at all, but I decided to do so because it provided me with yet another tool in my personal advancement toolbox.

At the time, all I knew about angels was what you would expect: they are messengers from god in the Abrahamic faith, that they serve roles or functions, that some are more powerful than others, that they're often times harbingers, and that initially they came from Zoroastrianism and were carried over into the beliefs of Abraham. From there it was all internal gnosis work and internal reconciliation.

I didn't want to be one of 'those people' who won't work with something because they've got an emotional tie to said subject. I get it, and I was that way for a couple of decades of my life, however, the older I get, the more I see the wisdom in moving on.

Did you catch what I said above? When I started this adventure, I knew angels didn't come from Christianity, rather that they were from a pre-existing belief system called Zoroastrianism, so I knew they weren't Abrahamic, if you want to split hairs.

In order to fulfill a Dion Fortune axiom, I decided to research them to the fullest, because, after all, 'the nearer the source, the purer the stream'. This is where things got *very* interesting, as the research has proven to yield fruit after fruit of lost knowledge.

I often say that everything in the western tradition comes back to Egypt, although usually I say it in jest. However, what time, experience, and research are routinely telling me is that most of the western tradition is from ancient Egypt. For example, angels. In the collection of papyri known as the *Pyramid Texts*, there are references that translate to the equivalent of what we would know as angels. Angels of Thoth, (Unas text, line 191) and other similar concepts can be occasionally found in various papyri that constitute the *Pyramid Texts*, which date back to approximately 2000 BCE. I did not expect to find references there, but I did. Nothing happens in a vacuum though, and I decided to look at what else was going on in the area, because Egypt influenced others, and others influenced Egypt.

After finding this nugget of wisdom, I decided to look further, and what I found filled in the gaps, which I then cut with Occam's Razor. Akhenaton was ruling Egypt, preaching monotheism at around the same time that the Hebrew people left Egypt.

There are many theories behind these two events, one of which being that Akhenaton, who fled Egypt due to public outcry, was in fact Moses, the leader of the Hebrew people at that time. I won't go into all of the theories here, I simply want to show the rise of monotheism, and how it stems back to Egypt.

When the Hebrew people left Egypt, they are said to have wandered the desert for 40 years, and would logically have run into other people in the area who had their own beliefs. One of the deities that was popular at the time was a storm deity named Yahweh, with whom they identified strongly, and would eventually take on as part of their own spiritual paradigm.

Settling and eventually building their own kingdom, the Hebrew people had interactions with these same people, and many other cultures. Some of these people would have been the indigenous people of the area and their beliefs. Some of these groups would have been the groups who had beliefs that would eventually become Zoroastrianism, which, if you'll remember, was my initial belief as to the origins of angels. Thus, it became clear that angels existed in ancient Egypt, and that they existed in ancient Persian beliefs, too. The Zoroastrian view is clearly defined, and when we look at their beliefs, we can see how they were the precursor to Abrahamic beliefs.

Tracing this further, we widen our scope to the ancient city of Babylon, and we find that the Hebrew and Egyptian people both had extensive trade and relations with the city. This is key to note because Babylon was the crossroads for a lot of different cultures, and thus, a lot of concepts and ideas were exchanged there and transmitted along trade routes that would eventually become the Silk Road. This exchange wasn't just relegated to physical goods, it also encompassed spiritual beliefs and concepts. It is through this common connection point that the idea of angels began to take firm root due to the rise of Zoroastrianism. I won't go too much into the historical side of Zoroastrianism here due to brevity, but there are a few key concepts of the faith I would like to point out.

At this point it is wise to remember that the Hebrew belief system had been firmly in place for several centuries, while Christianity wasn't even a gleam in the eye of the cosmos. To put it bluntly, this was the age of the Torah, the first five books of the Old Testament of the Christian Bible, so we can get an understanding of the timeframe. This was also around the time of the rise of Mithraism, another Persian-based belief system that was rising in prominence.

However, this wasn't the Mithraism that was found in later Roman times, rather it was a precursor to it, mostly in name only, though. Let us resume our look at both for further information about angels, so we don't get ahead of ourselves. The core concept that Zoroastrianism gives us that was carried forward into the Abrahamic faiths is that there is a monotheistic god that is the source of all good, and there is a monotheistic adversary that is the source of all evil. The Earth is the battleground between the forces of good and the forces of evil, and the currency being traded and used is human souls, so each side is fighting for human souls. Also, part of this doctrine taught that each person has a guardian angel that protects and guides them throughout their life, and that beings that we can consider angels, for all intents and purposes, are basically the foot soldiers of each side.

So entrenched were these ideas of duality, god and the adversary, the Earth as a battleground, and angels on both sides, that references to them show up continually for centuries.

One of the pieces of evidence for this is a gnostic text found in the *Dead Sea Scrolls* called *The War of the Sons of Light against the Sons of Darkness*, dated to approximately two centuries before the birth of Jesus the Christ.

To further prove this point, the first reference of an angel in the Judeo-Christian Bible occurs in the *Old Testament Book of Daniel*, which was written approximately one hundred years before the birth of Jesus the Christ. Linearly, what this means is that at this point, the belief in angels had already been around for several centuries before the Hebrew people were influenced by it, let alone before Christianity incorporated it.

The Hebrew mystic sect known as the Merkabah Movement gave structure to angels around this time, and this is important because it was the first time that material about the angels was structured and worked with in any particular way.

To complete the picture, what Mithraism gave to angelology is an early form of a solar phallic god, thus providing the idea that god is equivalent to light, and if angels come from god, then by default they come from light, or are at least of it. Mithraism was so strong that it got revived in Roman times but was distinctly different to its Persian predecessor.

Eventually all of this would filter down to Christianity, and would be added to until the Renaissance, when we have the addition of the feathered prater-human imagery that survives to this day to remind us of the changes that angels have undergone over the last four thousand years. Thus, what this tells us is that angels, and working with angels, is actually quite a Pagan practice, and predates Abrahamic faiths by centuries.

When I figured all of this out, things clicked together, and I was able to see the big picture. This allowed me to undo my programming, and to see that no matter the culture, this idea of fiery beings that can be both beneficial and benevolent has been around for a very long time, and thus, a lot of energy is built up in them to tap into.

So, there I was, at the healing point, and that's where the real healing began. Since the time of that epiphany, I have taken to working with angels to the degree that I have heavily explored the Enochian system of magick, and have even written extensively of angels, both in classes and books. It first required that I come to terms with it, and I found that through my research, I was able to see what these things are, and how I could work with them from a more magical perspective. This has proven to truly be a message from the gods that I cherish every day, and it is my hope you have the same success and can do the same.

APPENDIX IV
LOST ZODIACS

Throughout history there have been many interpretations and structures of the zodiac. None of which have been integrated into modern astrology, and most are considered evolutionary dead ends by professional astrologers. Usually, they are confined to, or inspired by, various magical grimoires, which is where you will find the most, albeit limited, information about them. Many times, these systems still have validity to them, but limited power. This is not a criticism of them, rather it is an accurate interpretation of thoughtforms and egregores.

As many of you know, the more attention and energy that is paid to something, the more power is generated and available for use. So, as we see in common society today, the bigger the idea, the more power it has, and thus the more effective it is to work with. Conversely, the smaller the idea, or the fewer people invested in it, the less powerful it is, and the weaker the results. This doesn't mean there are no results, rather that they manifest in smaller ways. These lost zodiacs can be seen as the latter, effective if worked with, but smaller in manifestation.

I share all of this to let you know that you can work with these systems, however, don't expect big results.

I find this a very interesting field of study because unlike most professional astrologers, I am also an occultist, enjoying ritual magick from a dusty grimoire as much as the ceremonial magician. Learning about astrological correlations between angels, demons, and the signs of astrology is fascinating to me, but so is discovering forgotten systems and bits of wisdom that time swallowed.

In the well-known grimoire *The Lesser Key of Solomon the King*, astrological correspondences to demons are listed. This is just one example of many, and with some time devoted to research, you will discover many other nuances running through the grimoiric tradition.

Not all astrological systems are confined to old grimoires, there are some that have simply withered and died rather than being absorbed or discarded. It should also be noted that thousands of years ago the astronomical constellations and astrological signs were one and the same. As a matter of fact, this alignment is where the astrological signs got their names and starting points.

Now however, thanks to the precession of the equinoxes, astrological signs and astronomical constellations are no longer the same. I'll say it again, just to be clear. Constellations are NOT the same as signs, even though they share many of the same names. This is because over time, there has been a drift that occurred for several reasons.

Approximately two thousand years ago, the constellation Aries rose on the eastern horizon at spring equinox in the northern hemisphere, however, in the present day, Pisces rises at the same spot and time.

Astrologers learned this long before astronomy even existed and knew that in order for it to continue to be relevant and effective, something had to be done about it. Of course, they knew they couldn't change the properties of the planet that caused this, so instead, the sky was divided into twelve equal sections, and the names of the constellations were carried over, because there was already substantial energy within them and familiarity with them.

It should also be kept in mind that these are not mutually exclusive. You can work with both the constellations and zodiacal signs when it comes to your ritual work.

A common practice is to incorporate the constellation Orion into ritual work because of its correspondence to the hunt, whether it is the thrill of the hunt or the hunter themselves.

A creative magician or witch can overlap the traits of both into a more effective, potent ritual. Psychologically, one of the things that is subconsciously occurring is the blending of astrology and astronomy. This is an idea that has been coming into being over the last few decades, as more astrologers embrace astronomical concepts. Unfortunately, astronomers are not doing the same, and until they do, we will not achieve healing.

Anyway, back to the zodiac I will look at here. This material is taken from an astrological kit called *The Lost Zodiac* by Catherine Tennant. In it she discusses the signs of a lost zodiac. Technically, what she is doing is addressing an older approach to astrology before the great thinker Ptolemy came along and simplified astrology down to twelve signs. To clarify, the word zodiac means belt of beasts, and refers to the signs located along the ecliptic in outer space. In this way, the zodiac encircles the Earth. To the educated mind, there are more stars and constellations at the ecliptic than the twelve signs used in astrology. In earlier systems, all of these were incorporated into astrology.

The most recent example of this is the uproar and disinformation about Ophiuchus. Many years ago, an uneducated astronomer tried to insert that constellation into astrology, and as expected, it failed spectacularly because the astrological community came out to clarify that it is not inserted into astrology, it makes no sense to insert it into astrology, and frankly, the whole media spectacle is proof positive of the ignorance of the astronomical community regarding astrological matters.

The problem that came with this is that the media exposure led to confusion for the average person who only knows astrology at a passing glance. That was where the damage was done.

Regardless, the astronomer was right, albeit anachronistic. In earlier renditions of astrology, Ophiuchus, other constellations and fixed stars were looked at along with the constellations that would eventually become signs. This is the essence of the lost zodiac.

Here we will take a closer look at a dead-end in astrology. Keep in mind that just because modern astrology does not integrate these with regular signs, it doesn't mean they can't be worked with to a large degree when it comes to your ritual magick.

As we go through the material below, I will also point out the festivals that align with these stellar phenomena so that you have enough preliminary material to work with as you see fit, if you decide to at all. Enough of the background material. Let's go!

Below are dates of governance, which should be familiar to those with an interest in astrology. A constellation is listed, as are stars. Many of the stars have survived over the centuries and are not considered fixed by modern astrologers. Fixed stars are those that move much more slowly than the planets. The word planet means wanderer, and its etymology tells us that centuries ago it was noticed that some lights in the night sky moved faster than others. Over time these were identified as the planets, with the slower-moving stars being considered fixed. Technically they are not fixed, rather they move so much more slowly than the planets that for all practical purposes they are stationary.

To wit, fixed stars move approximately one degree every seventy-two years, whereas most of the seven ancient planets move approximately one degree a day. Fixed stars have properties, as the planets do, but their effects are not as pronounced or dynamic. They are considered background material, whereas the planets are foreground.

I won't give properties for the constellations as they mostly come from Greco-Roman myth, and are therefore easy to learn, but I will include correspondences for the fixed stars for your reference and application.

DATES	CONSTELLATION	FIXED STAR(S)	FIXED STAR(S) TRAITS
DEC 29 - JAN 13	THE LYRE OF ORPHEUS	VEGA	VENUS AND MERCURY
JAN 14 - JAN 28	THE EAGLE	ALTAIR	MARS AND JUPITER
JAN 29 - FEB 8	THE DOLPHIN	ROTANEV & SUALOCIN	SATURN AND MARS
FEB 9 - FEB 29	CYGNUS	SADR	SATURN MINUS VENUS
MAR 1 - MAR 12	THE RIVER OF NIGHT	ACHERNAR	JUPITER
MAR 13 - APR 1	PEGASUS	MARKAB, SCHEAT, ALGENIB	MERCURY AND MARS
APR 2 - APR 9	ANDROMEDA	ALPHERATZ	JUPITER AND VENUS
APR 10 - APR 18	THE RIVER OF NIGHT	ACAMAR	VENUS
APR 19 - MAY 8	ANDROMEDA	MIRACH, ALMACH	SATURN (MIRACH), VENUS AND MARS (ALMACH)
MAY 9 - MAY 15	THE RIVER OF NIGHT	RANA, ZAURAK	SATURN
MAY 16 - MAY 31	PERSEUS	ALGOL, MIRFAK	SATURN AND JUPITER
JUNE 1 - JUNE 7	ORION	RIGEL	MARS AND JUPITER
JUNE 8 - JUNE 16	THE CHARIOTEER	CAPELLA	MARS AND MERCURY
JUNE 17 - JUNE 27	ORION	BETELGEUSE	MARS WITH SLIGHT MERCURY
JUNE 28 - JULY 7	THE DOGS	SIRIUS	JUPITER AND MARS

Table 3. Lost constellations and fixed star correspondences.

Table 4. Continuation of Table 3

JULY 8 – JULY 17	THE SHIP OF THE ARGONAUTS	CANOPUS	SATURN AND JUPITER
JULY 18 – JULY 25	THE DOGS	PROCYON	MERCURY WITH SLIGHT MARS
JULY 26 – AUG 7	THE DRAGON	GIANFAR	SOUTH NODE OF THE MOON
AUG 8 – AUG 15	THE GREAT BEAR	DUBHE, MERAK	MARS AND MERCURY (DUBHE), VENUS (MERAK)
AUG 16 – AUG 23	THE SEA SERPENT	ALPHARD	SATURN AND VENUS, OR SUN SEXTILE JUPITER
AUG 24 – SEPT 10	THE GREAT BEAR	PHECDA, MEGREZ, ALIOTH, MIZAR	VENUS (PHECDA), MARS (MEGREZ), VENUS (ALIOTH), VENUS (MIZAR)
SEPT 11 – SEPT 21	THE CUP	ALKES	NEPTUNE
SEPT 22 – SEPT 28	THE SHIP OF THE ARGONAUTS	MARKAB	MERCURY AND MARS
SEPT 29 – OCT 11	THE RAVEN	MINKAR, ALGORAB	MARS AND SATURN
OCT 12 – OCT 26	THE BEAR KEEPER	ARCTURUS, IZAR	JUPITER AND MARS (ARCTURUS), MARS (IZAR)
OCT 27 – NOV 10	THE CROWN OF THE NORTH WIND	ALPHECCA	VENUS AND THE SUN
NOV 11 – NOV 19	THE SERPENT	UNUKALHAI	MARS
NOV 20 – DEC 5	THE WISE CENTAUR	ALPHA CENTAURI	VENUS AND JUPITER
DEC 6 – DEC 16	OPHIUCHUS	HAN, SABIK, RAS ALHAGUE	MOON, JUPITER TO A LESSER DEGREE (HAN), VENUS (SABIK), SATURN WITH NEGATIVE VENUS (RAS ALHAGUE)
DEC 17 – DEC 23	THE DRAGON	GRUMIUM, ELTANIN	SATURN AND MARS
DEC 24 – DEC 28	THE SERPENT	ALYA	SATURN AND MARS

You can see that for each of the fixed stars, or group of stars, their traits are usually seen as being of a nature similar to another planet's characteristics. This is a technique that has been used since time immemorial, because it is easier to apply what you know about the planets to the fixed stars we're discussing here. The fixed stars have more specific traits and characteristics than the broad traits of the planets they reference, but I left those details out due to space. More information can easily be found about the fixed stars in various books and websites, such as astrologyking.com. Each of the fixed stars are found in a particular constellation, which also means they are located in particular signs, so the seasoned astrologer can look to see where these fixed stars are in their natal charts and get further insight into how those planets will play out through the course of one's life.

Pertaining to our conversation, let's apply these fixed stars to their wheel of the year festival correspondence. For the sake of brevity and ease, I will use the calendar dates for the festivals, and once you master that you can move on to the astrological timing of the festivals. The following chart shows which fixed signs are present at which festivals, and thus gives you the ability to further detail and empower your rituals.

FESTIVAL	FIXED STAR	FIXED STAR PLANETARY INFLUENCES
IMBOLC FEBRUARY 1	ROTANEV & SUALOCIN	SATURN AND MARS
SPRING EQUINOX	MARKAB, SCHEAT, ALGENIB	MERCURY AND MARS
BELTANE MAY 1	MIRACH, ALMACH	SATURN (MIRACH), VENUS AND MARS (ALAMACH)
SUMMER SOLSTICE	BETELGEUSE	MARS WITH SLIGHT MERCURY
LUGHNASADH AUGUST 1	GIANFAR	SOUTH NODE OF THE MOON
AUTUMN EQUINOX	ALKES, MARKAB	NEPTUNE, MERCURY AND MARS (DEPENDS ON THE DAY)
SAMHAIN NOVEMBER 1	ALPHECCA	VENUS AND THE SUN
WINTER SOLSTICE	GRUMIUM, ELTANIN	SATURN AND MARS

Table 5. Wheel of the Year festivals and fixed stars.

The previous chart is based on the northern hemisphere, so adjust accordingly if you live in the southern. One of the ways you can work with this information is to integrate the traits of the fixed stars into your rituals, whether through decoration, invocations, or intentions. There are many other ways, of course, but these are good starting points if you want to go this route. Another point to note is that the knowledge of these fixed stars and their prevalence can tell you why a ritual went one way during one festival, but a different way on the following year's. You can also determine this by looking at planetary placements, however, remember that the fixed stars are the background, and it is because of this that their manifestations are subtler.

Another approach you can take is to incorporate the constellations into your rituals rather than the fixed stars themselves. There is a rich history for each constellation in the sky, and these histories vary from culture to culture. With a little research you can discover their traits for your spiritual paradigm. For example, the constellation Orion is usually viewed through the lens of its namesake, but we can look at it through an Egyptian lens, where Horus corresponds to the constellation, and if you prefer, you can look at the constellation through the outdated lens of it corresponding to Osiris.

Some of the fixed stars may already be familiar to you such as Sirius, while others may be more obscure. Not every fixed star has the same amount of information on it, and I point this out because you might be challenged to find information to work with for some stars, while others have ample amounts of material, so take this into account before the festival itself. Using fixed stars during festival rituals is not a last-minute decision.

As I said at the beginning, the above system is simply one of several that have been buried beneath the sands of time, so if you come across something in your research, then by all means explore it. It can help you personalize your work, but it should not be meant as a replacement for regular astrology.

The creative person can use the discovered system and standard astrology together for greater personalization and empowerment. I don't want to dissuade you from other minor astrological systems, rather give you context for what you find during your journeys.

Another example is the Dendera zodiac. This is the famous Egyptian zodiac from the temple to Hathor at Dendera Egypt. This is an example of another forgotten zodiac, more specifically, one that was ultimately absorbed into common astrology today.

We know it existed, and it has power and validity, but what is not taken into account is context. The temple of Dendera dates from later times in ancient Egypt, so relatively speaking it is not that old. Hence, the information it has was not necessarily true during the majority of the reign of the empire, which lasted thousands of years. In earlier dynasties and kingdoms, multiple astrological systems existed, and were used concurrently. There was a lunar calendar that was mostly used for religious and spiritual timing, while the solar calendar was generally used for the more administrative and social sides of civilization. When we connect the dots, we see that how ancient Egyptians viewed the stars changed dramatically, and with Dendera we see a marked influence from Mesopotamia and Greece. The redeeming trait is that it was common for ancient Egyptian temples to be built on top of each other, so even though the zodiac at Dendera is newer, it is most likely and logically built at the same temple site of previous astrology work. This means Dendera did not come out of a vacuum, rather it shows both Egyptian and foreign influences. While I am not interested in that, I know many who are, and personally, I know it a decent amount and enjoy using it. I just keep in mind that it is not purely Egyptian, but it sure is nice to be fluent in it for sheer pleasure and flavor in my spiritual paradigm.

A third example is the Celtic Tree zodiac, also known as the Druid zodiac. In short, it corresponds each astrological sign to a particular tree, especially those connected with Celtic culture. Personally, I like it, but it receives a heavy dose of scrutiny when it comes to its authenticity. Frankly, I think it's all rubbish, I also don't really care. It's accurate as it is, and I'm not one to get caught up in that debate. If it works, it works, and that is all there is to it, historicity be damned. I won't get into this system as much as I did Dendera, I mention it here as an example of a system that is a somewhat modern construction, yet still provides information as valid as what you might find from any amateur astrologer, of which there are many. I could go on and on with examples of alternative astrological systems, but I will stop for now. I'm sure my point is clear, as is the point to go out and explore. Enjoy exploring these various systems, just keep in mind the context.

APPENDIX V
SYMBOLIC PATTERNS IN ASTROLOGY

If you want to enhance what you're doing, ritualistically or otherwise, but you don't know where to look, astrology can help you fine-tune imagery and other metaphysical understandings to increase your effectiveness and power. Here I will talk about a few different observations that you can include in your seasonal practices.

Each season is comprised of three astrological signs. While the signs may vary, the astrological modalities do not. In astrology, each sign has a quality. It is a pattern of manifestation that occurs when it comes to the affairs of that sign.

There are three modalities: cardinal, fixed, and mutable. In older times the word common was used instead of mutable. This is just a point of reference for those of you who read older astrological books. Cardinal signs are those that are initiatory, forward thinking, and progressive. Fixed astrological signs are those that are steadier, preferring routine and sometimes discipline. Consistency is what matters. Mutable signs are those that are fluid and adaptable.

So, each season has these components to it. It generally comes in with a bang (cardinal), stabilizes (fixed), and rapidly fluctuates as the next season arrives (mutable) and the current one ends. This is the same pattern every season.

When you're timing your festival work, it is wise to take this into account. If you are executing a ritual at the beginning of a season (solstices and equinoxes, then the dominant energy is forward-thinking and progressive (cardinal). If you are executing one of the fire festivals during the heart of the season, the energy is more reflective of the status quo. I have found this particularly useful because it reminds me that initiations and all things related to moving forward are better saved for the solstices and equinoxes, whereas rituals that have to do with maintaining the status quo and stability are better done during the fire festivals.

There is a particular pattern and rhythm to the elements of the signs, which is not only good to keep in mind when timing rituals, it is also when learning astrology. Let's start with Aries, the first sign in the zodiac. It is the cardinal fire sign. It is followed by Taurus, the fixed earth sign, then Gemini, the mutable air sign. So, we have the pattern of fire, earth, and then air.

The next season begins with Cancer, which is the cardinal water sign. Notice how both Aries and Cancer begin the next season? This is correct, cardinal signs start seasons, and there is one cardinal sign per element. Following Cancer is the fixed fire sign Leo, which is followed by the mutable earth sign Virgo, which in turn is followed by the cardinal air sign Libra ... and the pattern continues: fire, earth, air, water, fire, earth, air, water, and so on. You can see how each elemental sign drops down a position during each season, i.e., fire is the first element in spring, the second element in summer, and the third element in autumn.

During spring, earth is the second sign, in the summer, it is the third, and in the winter, it is the first, only to become second the following spring, and the cycle repeats.

When you look at these two points, you see there is a rhythm to the astrological wheel and also to the wheel of the year itself.

A rhythm of the wheel of the year is obvious to most casual observers, and the astrological sublimity is worth noting because the real power is revealed through the imagery. Allow me to explain.

Spring is comprised of three signs: Aries, Taurus, and Gemini. The imagery for these are the ram, the bull, and the human twins, respectively. This means that when you're looking at the spring festivals (Ostara and Beltane), it would be wise to incorporate imagery and symbolism that have to do with horns, whether it is the horned god or something else of your own design. Two of the three signs are bestial, while the third is human. This tells us that the dominant symbolism is bestial.

Summer is comprised of the crab, the lion, and the human virginal woman. There's no strong imagery here like there is during spring with the horns, but what we find is that two of the three signs are feminine, telling us that the nature of summer is more feminine than masculine.

Autumn is comprised of the scales, the scorpion, the serpent, the phoenix, the eagle, and the centaur. There is no common thread like there was in spring or summer, what we have instead is the season that has the most imagery attached to it. This is largely due to the adaptability of Scorpio, which encompasses four animals (serpent, scorpion, phoenix, eagle), but Libra doesn't even have a beast or human for symbolism, rather it has an abstract symbol.

Finally, the centaur is technically not a flesh and blood creature, but is here, nonetheless. This tells us that with autumn, unlike any other system, we find the fantastical, the creatures and ideas that go beyond the black and white animal-human conflict we all endure until death. Personally, I feel like this makes autumn the most magical season, but that is just me looking at it from a purely astrological perspective.

Finally, winter is comprised of the goat, the sea goat, the energy bearer, and the two fishes. We see a touch of the mystical during the season of winter with the imagery of the sea goat, otherwise this season is comprised of the classic conflict between beast and man, just like spring and summer.

In this way, not only is it a return to normality, it is also a bridge to the repeating season of spring, on the horizon, which is the time of the horned god.

You can blend the qualities of the modalities and the imagery of the signs to great effect, bringing better, more accurate symbolism into your rituals, and connecting with beings you might not have considered otherwise.

An unintentional selling point that I'm sure you've seen is that of autumn, with its sense of wonder and the magical, it is also worth mentioning that sometimes you want your festival rituals to simply go smoothly and maintain the status quo.

Whatever your intention is, the fact of the matter remains that what I discuss here can increase the potency and results of your sympathetic magic rituals during the eight-spoked Wheel of the Year, the sacred festivals that have endured for centuries and will endure for many more.

BIBLIOGRAPHY
FOR FURTHER READING

Instead of the usual format, I am going to approach this from a broader perspective. The reason for this is because I have been walking this spiritual path for over thirty-five years, and it is impossible to chapter and verse everything I've read and learned over the years. Couple this with the fact that this subject is so popular that books on the festivals and wheel in general number in the hundreds if not thousands, and many of them have been in print for only a short time, making their accumulation difficult.

With effort, you can find at least one book, if not more, about the festivals and the wheel in general that aligns with your spiritual paradigm and beliefs. Many books over the decades have regurgitated the same material in either countless editions or by various authors for whatever reasons, so rather than introduce you to a long list of books that are repetitive, I will introduce you to highlights to consider when researching the festivals.

When building your collection of wheel of the year books, the place to start is with reference books.

Doreen Valiente's *An ABC of Witchcraft* comes to mind, as does *Encyclopedia of Wicca & Witchcraft* by Raven Grimassi, both of which I consulted when putting this book together. Two other reference books that were highly valuable were *The Witches' God* and *The Witches' Goddess*, both by Janet and Stewart Farrar. They also wrote *A Witches' Bible*, which I cannot recommend highly enough. All three of their books form a wonderful system of value to both the beginner and advanced practitioner. Multiple times, Llewellyn Publishing has released specialized books on each of the festivals, so those are out there, too.

Another highly specialized book that illustrates how specific you can get regarding seasonal and festival practices is *The Equinox & Solstice Ceremonies of the Golden Dawn*, by Pat & Chris Zalewski (Llewellyn Publishing, 1992). If the Hermetic Order of the Golden Dawn is not your paradigm, then you can skip this book, but it does go to show that there are specialty books out there for many spiritual traditions and how they approach the various festivals of the year.

Another good place to start that can help you understand and work with the eight seasonal festivals is history. This can be broken down into two categories: 1) The history of the festivals and wheel as we know them, and 2) Cultural folklore. Let's take a closer look.

Many books have been released over the last fifty years that detail history and contemporary perspectives on the wheel of the year, so I will keep our conversation focused on recent books.

Two must-reads to explore where we have come from over the last forty years are *Drawing Down the Moon* by Margot Adler, and *The Spiral Dance* by Starhawk. Some of the material in them is dated, however most of their contents can give you some insight into how we got to where we are, a quarter of the way through the twenty-first century. *The Power of the Witch* by Laurie Cabot also comes to mind in this category. These are just a few more popular examples, but many others also exist.

For history, there are two I strongly recommend, and were quite valuable when writing this book. The first is *The Triumph of the Moon* by Professor Ronald Hutton. In my opinion, there is no better book on the subject. Professor Hutton goes into so much detail and with such clarity that you can read it time and again and pick up on something new each time. *Modern Wicca* by Michael Howard is close, although it is more contemporary in nature, whereas Hutton's book is timeless.

The second book I suggest is *Christianity: The Origins of a Pagan Religion* by Philippe Walter.

This one is of particular interest for our purposes because it goes into specifics when it comes to how these festivals got their starts. In it, he walks us through several centuries of history and shows how the roots of the festivals lie in the traveling carnival, quite common in those times. There are many other books on the history of the craft and thus the wheel of the year, but Hutton and Walter's books command attention when assessing details and history.

When it comes to folklore, that is another story. I don't have specific books to recommend to you because this is such a niche subject, and the study of folklore has been around far longer than the study of Neopaganism, where the wheel of the year is most commonly found today. There are even folklore societies in various countries that study such material, and many of them have nothing to do with the wheel of the year as it is today.

However, you can find information on seasonal rites that are essentially based on what we have been talking about, that align with your culture, whether national or ethnic. More than just books, folklore also encompasses local traditional practices that have never been written about before, or at least very minimally.

For example, it has only been recently that I discovered a local high school has a Maypole practice dating back about a hundred years, and the only people that know about it are those who are or were in the area, or who participated in it. In short, it is not really discussed for obvious reasons, to do with religious bigotry.

While I lived in Poland, I read a few books on Polish folklore to learn about the culture and discovered many of them covered essentially Pagan practices that aligned with the seasons or other Neopagan concepts. You would never see this mentioned in the books because Poland is ninety-five percent Catholic.

This illustrates the point I am making. While most books on folklore are not overt when it comes to their connection to the wheel of the year, an educated reader will find much information that can be of great value for their ritual work. These stories may be tainted by later religious influence, however, the astute reader will be able to sift through this veneer to find the pearls of wisdom contained.

I hope this untraditional look at recommended books and further reading helps you during your journey.

Most of all, follow your intuition when it comes to further reading, although temper that with Occam's Razor, after all, too often people try to make connections that are not there.

www.ingramcontent.com/pod-product-compliance
Lightning Source LLC
Chambersburg PA
CBHW070655120526
44590CB00013BA/975